The Potless Pot High

How to Get High

Clear and Spunky

Without Weed

Other Books by Bear Jack Gebhardt

(See them all on Amazon.com)

- *How to Stop Smoking in 15 Easy Years*
  A Slacker's Guide to Final Freedom
- *Happy John: An Advaita (Non-Duality) Gospel*
- *Practicing the Presence of Peace*
- *The Enlightened Smoker's Guide to Quitting*
- *How to Help Your Smoker Quit*
- *Now Hiring* (with Steve Lauer)

The Potless Pot High

How to Get High, Clear and Spunky without Weed

Going Beyond Marijuana:

5 Games to Play to Catch a Daily Buzz

Bear Jack Gebhardt

Seven Traditions Press

Bellevue, Colorado

 Published 2013

First Edition

ISBN: 978-1-938651-04-5

Library of Congress: Number: 2013915179

Printed in the United States of America

For all you midnight tokers …

Contents

Contents (cont)

Chapter 1: The First Head Rush

Is There Really Such a Thing as a *Potless Pot High?*

(otherwise known as *Weedless Enlightenment?)*

Fearing I'll die
holding a toke
I always exhale
with a smile.

---Raskin Olikov

When asked "What is enlightenment," the Buddha responded, "Enlightenment is the end of suffering."

The end of suffering? Let's vote: All in favor? All opposed?

We smoke weed basically to end the suffering, start the pleasuring, get enlightened. And it obviously works, to a degree. Otherwise we wouldn't do it. Duh.

As someone who, as with many in my generation, first starting smoking and enjoying weed before I was legally old enough to drink, and whose hair is now mostly white, I've also naturally been searching for practical alternatives along the way. The herb high is righteous---that's why millions of us indulge it. Wouldn't it be even better to be that buzzed without the hassle? Of course.

So, in my ordinary day-life I've been casually experimenting, testing, practicing and refining various insights and approaches that might lead to a daily buzz, e.g.

a *potless pot high,* or a *weedless enlightenment.* I've been searching for how to be high, clear and spunky without the use of pot, since I already know how to do it using pot.

I've compared my experience with these "potless" games --these get-high techniques and insights-- against my experience with the actual use of pot to see how they match up, how the highs match up. I want the real thing, not just a watered down, politically correct, sheriff-approved version.

Here's my quest: Is it possible to stay high, to stay happy and peaceful, buzzed, or at least at ease, without the use of weed? Is it possible to stay grinning, loving, insightful and kind --- stay happy, grinning --- from the time I wake up in the morning to the time I go to sleep? Sounds impossible, and yet . . .

The reason I'm on this quest is both practical and personal: I've discovered it's a lot more fun, a lot more healthy, and even much more profitable to be high rather than low, happy rather than sad, clear rather than foggy, spunky rather than punchy, or couch potato-ed. If Buddha said enlightenment is the end of suffering. I suggest it's better to be enlightened than to be suffering! (Again, duh.)

I know first-hand that smoking pot tends to end the suffering. But it has some downsides, the most irritating of which is that you keep coming down. And, oh yeah, it's been illegal for most of my life and thus fairly expensive and sometimes hard to obtain. So this book shares some of the adventures I've had and the techniques and insights I've picked up in my own forty-year quest for a *potless* way of attaining the same high, of being naturally happy, peaceable, even "unshakably comfortable" in my own skin, in my own ordinary life. I've found that the "high games" I now play every day actually do work to keep me high, end the suffering, start the giggling. They are frighteningly simple games, easy to learn and, in fact, quite natural, though not yet very common or widely used.

I assume my reader friends have their own ordinary lives with which they have likewise been experimenting to end the suffering, start the grinning, with and without pot. I trust this book will help expand and deepen the experiments already ongoing.

This book is not an argument for a particular belief system or outlined way of life. Rather it's an invitation to the reader to test in his or her own daily life whether what I have found (so far) does indeed generate a real potless pot high, a weedless enlightenment, the end of suffering. If it does, I'd like to hear about it. If it doesn't, I'd like to hear about that, too. We're voyagers here, sharing what's in our knapsacks.

Nevertheless, even though we can share our findings, by its very nature this quest for a potless pot high turns out to be a mostly private, personal, quite subtle inner journey. Of course, part of the joy, the pleasuring is sharing the buzz with family and friends, and learning from them, their own best steps. Still, during most of our days, it's something we have to do on our own.

Over the years I've offered numerous "first tokes," so to speak, of these potless pot high games to friends and clients, sharing my discoveries, and offering gentle guidance on this potless, get-high process. And they likewise have shared their discoveries with me. Although it seems we often suffer alone, it appears we don't come to an end of suffering just for ourselves. **When suffering ends for us, it ends for those around us, both near and far, at least to a degree**.

A Brief Personal History

Let's back up a minute. As should be obvious by now, I'm not afraid or embarrassed to admit that I used to smoke pot almost every day, sometimes morning and night, simply because I enjoyed the effect. I liked what pot did to my thinking and feeling and to the new way I paid attention to the world after I'd smoked. I enjoyed getting high, used to say the only reason I would ever *not* smoke pot was because I'd found a better way to get there (here.)

For many years, most of my friends were also pot smokers, and included doctors, lawyers, architects, school teachers, nurses, businessmen, psychologists, and caring, loving, attentive mothers and fathers. (And a few burned out pot head bums.) I know, as mentioned, that the two biggest problems with pot are: 1.) it's mostly illegal; and 2). we keep coming down.

So, with that said, it should be clear that this book is not for everyone. If you're an old millennium lock-em-up-and-throw-away-the-key type of person when it comes to pot use, this book is probably not for you. You'll probably feel very challenged, your mind fences breached, and thus be made uncomfortable by many of the basic assumptions and attitudes herein expressed.

I myself am quite at ease with the topic, just as an old time bricklayer is at ease with his bricks and scaffolding, though ever-mindful that there's always much more to learn. I've been up and down these ladders (so to speak) most of my life. And destiny and good fortune led me to devote much of my adult career to the professional "substance abuse" business, helping folks walk away from hard core drug and alcohol addictions and, lately, the most hard core of all, tobacco addiction. I've written three books on tobacco addiction and delivered papers at fancy universities and national conferences. But most of my time was spent leading one to one and group counseling sessions, helping folks get a grip (or loosen their grip, as the case often happens to be) on their addictions.

But let's be clear: **this is *not* a recovery from pot book**! This is a how to get high, clear and spunky without weed book. Like I said, the two biggest problems with pot are that 1.) we keep coming down and 2.) it's illegal. The second problem is becoming less and less of a problem. (I'm happy to report that as I write, in the state of Washington and here in Colorado, where I live, smoking pot for either medicinal or recreational purposes is no longer illegal, due to a popular vote. It's been a long time coming. Let's hope the tide is changing.)

Of course, other than its illegality, there are a few other, more minor problems with pot use--a certain giggly ADD is one example, and the *manana* syndrome can be another, and it is a bit rough on the lungs. But the *high itself,* as millions of folks can attest, can often be perfectly sweet, righteous.

The First Head Rush

Let's get to the reason behind this chapter's title: "The First Head Rush." Here's a quick little story: After researching various methods for a "potless pot high" and working on this book for many years, I was deep into what I was sure would be the "final first draft" when a couple of old buddies--one a successful lawyer, the other a successful architect--called on a Friday evening after they had quaffed a few beers at the pub.

My buds said they had some righteous herb. They invited me to join them. Not so many years ago such "substance enhanced" celebrations, with these and other buddies had been my regular practice. In recent years, however I had been politely declining such invitations—as I had earlier that evening declined joining them at the pub--because I've been less and less attracted to the old forms of celebration.

My long-time friendship with these gents was and still is deep and valuable. They too practice the "potless pot high" games, though perhaps not with the passion or regularity that I find myself indulging. That Friday evening, for some reason, probably something to do with wanting to test the "final first draft" of this book, I felt that the time, the place, the mood was again just right to indulge the herb. Besides, the wife was gone for the evening. I invited them over. When they arrived, we lit up.

Ahh shucks, I thought, shortly after my first toke, feeling the rush. (I didn't need more than a couple of tokes—it was indeed righteous weed, and, besides, I was already nicely high, thank you, before they arrived!)

Ahh shucks. I thought. Getting high with weed is completely different than the high that comes with the potless pot high games that I had been describing in my book. Shucks, I'd have to start all over.

And then, in a short while, I observed, no, the high experience that I was sharing and describing in this book is *not* different from the get-high from weed. The difference is only in the first head-rush.

"Every speed freak I know is basically trying to get back to that first rush," a lady friend (and speed freak) told me many decades ago. This is also true for many of the other get-high substances, including cocaine and heroin---but only partially true. (With weed, most folks need to *learn* to get high; there's generally not a real specific first rush.) Although the first rush with pot is, well—quite a rush---*being* high is more than just the thrill of the first rush, or the second or the third rush, even though, especially for young experimenters, that rush can be the first "catch."

As we'll discover in this book, there truly is something real, something necessary and even healthy about the get-high experience itself, or at least the feel-good experience. Feeling good does something to our neurological processes that is very nice and very natural. It's not just the first rush, though the quickness of moving our attention from here to there, moving our feelings from low to high, moving quickly from suffering to pleasuring is obviously a strong attraction for large numbers of people.

So, the good news, bad news:

Bad news first: The mental and emotional processes that you will find in this book that make up the potless pot high games do *not,* alas, give us a quick first rush, like the first couple of tokes of righteous weed will do. That's the bad news. Sorry. No first obvious head rush. That's just the way it is.

The good news is that these processes can, and do, offer a tiny, almost unnoticeable *little* rush. And unlike the big rushes we get from righteous weed, the little rushes that we get from the games outlined in *The Potless Pot High* stay with us. So as we engage these games day after day, we keep getting higher and higher. But also, thankfully, clearer and clearer, spunkier and spunkier. And surprise of surprises: we also become more and more grounded, and thus more efficient in our daily round of affairs. (As we know, that is *not* necessarily the experience we get from daily pot use.)

Intrigued? Hope so. But it seemed necessary to be clear up front about the lack of a "first head rush," (For some people, the fact that there is *no* big head rush in the potless pot high might be viewed as good news!) Admitting to this lack of a big head rush seemed honest and necessary in order to keep the jeers from my friends in the peanut gallery down to a low grumble. (I've heard it before: *"This must be ditch weed, dude—I don't get no rush")*

So here we go. I promise, if you keep toking, keep reading, you'll feel it. You'll get high.

Keep the Oreos handy.

Chapter 2
The Freedom Game:
The Basic Game of *The Potless Pot High*

"*Only the jailers are against escape.*"
--Wavy Gravy

Just watching kids at play anywhere in the world, we see that we human beings, when we are in our original state-- the state we experienced when we were kids--- are naturally high, naturally clear and spunky, free and easy. Isn't this how most of us felt, at least some of the time, even most of the time, when we were kids out playing--happy, free and easy?

One reason weed is so popular and in most ways perfectly healthy is that it seems to help us reconnect with this exact same free and easy state--connect with who we really are at heart.

So *The Potless Pot High* is simply one possible description of the result of playing any or all of the five games outlined in this book. Other words to describe that state might be "happy," or "easy," or "natural," or even, "somewhat enlightened." Isn't that how it feels to smoke pot, or to just feel like a kid again?

I know from my own direct experience and from the experience of those with whom I've shared these games that playing them does in fact lead to getting high and staying high, being happy, easy, natural, just as we felt when we were kids. The good news is that as adults we can do it much better than we did as kids, because as adults we know what we are doing, and have control over the process!

This book outlines a progressive series of simple, yet quite specific mental and emotional processes that we can engage, that lead to the free and easy get-high experience. We can play these games, if we so choose, in any circumstance and in every relationship. Which of the games we play may depend on which circumstance or relationship we're in at the moment. However, the single goal of the five different games is the same: being and staying high, clear and spunky.

As we move through our day we will most often play these games somewhat secretly, playing with our own thoughts and feelings and playing with our attention itself, with awareness itself. Unlike taking a bong hit in the judge's chamber, playing these get-high games will generally go unnoticed by others, though the effects are actually quite contagious. (People will get a contact high from you and not even know it!)

I am introducing the first, basic game, The Freedom Game, right here, in chapter two, without much background explanation, because we can *talk* about getting high all day long but that's not *getting* high.

The Wide Rainbow of Get-High Experiences

In later chapters, we'll look in more detail at the specifics of the marijuana high, and some of the findings from professional research in regard to changes in perception and changes in time/space cognitions and brain wave frequencies that occur with marijuana ingestion. But when it comes to the actual effects of marijuana use for *each individual,* we obviously have a wide rainbow of different experiences that people report at different times and places and with different grades of pot. Throw in the differences that occur between new users and long-time users, between rich people and poor people, between people with black, brown, red, white, or yellow skins (and cultures) and between healthy bodies and those bodies in need of medication, the difference between getting high on Friday night and Tuesday afternoon--with all these differences in "pot highs", the challenge of presenting a simple, yet comprehensive alternative becomes obvious.

Nevertheless, "how to get high without pot" is a delicious challenge, yes? A grin-inducing challenge. And even if the challenge is only partially met, we might agree it's still a worthy quest. And it's a quest that can be more enjoyable if we're a bit buzzed in the process. .

Some Basic Instructions: "*Just take it in, hold it as long as you can, then let it out.*"

One of the reasons I call this first game *The Freedom Game is* because that's what it does: it frees us up from the hum-drum of daily suffering--daily boredom, irritation and angst. (A bit like pot, yes?) As we know, it didn't take a whole lot of instruction or introduction to learn how to get high with pot. (*"Just take it in, hold it as long as you can, and let it out."*) Same with the potless pot high—it doesn't take a lot of instruction, but it does take some.

First, the game I'm about to describe--the Freedom Game--is done quite quickly. (Indeed, much quicker than smoking a bowl!) My description here of "how to do it" will take much longer than it takes to actually do it. Even though the game is played quickly, it needs to be played, when necessary or appropriate, again and again until it becomes natural.

Next, as I mentioned in the last chapter, when we first start practicing the Freedom Game we generally don't experience that first "rush" like we do with pot, and thus don't get as high, as fast, as when we smoke dope. (Again, I hear the folks in the peanut gallery: *Ahhh boo….*)

Don't let the lack of a head rush stop you from playing. It has been my experience that as we continue with the game--which, unlike pot, we can do while sitting in church or in our lawyer's office or at home with the folks or the kids--when we continue with the practice it becomes clear, over days and weeks, that the "pot high" elevation, the get-high experience can indeed be attained, and sustained, yet with much greater clarity and more energy than ever was available with weed. (*Yay!*)

And it happens without the often fuzzy, lethargic, sometimes irritable "pot hangover." So although we don't get as high when we first start, we do get as high, and higher in a relatively short amount of time (within days) and *stay* higher longer. So don't get discouraged in the first day or two.

Another forewarning: This first technique, *The Freedom Game*, may seem almost *too* simple. "Is that all there is?" It is indeed simple. Just as gathering a few leaves, setting them on fire and breathing in the smoke is simple. But it's like an onion-- the simplicity belies layer after layer within. It's *almost* too simple, until one tries it. "Things should be made as simple as possible," Einstein said, "but not simpler." This technique is simple, but not *too* simple.

And finally, you will discover that you *already know* this game, this technique. Kids do it naturally. *You* undoubtedly already do it, naturally, to one extent or another. The genius of Christian Alamyrac, M.D. the French physician who first invented ---or articulated--- the first basic form of the Freedom Game, was *not* that he came up with something completely new and unique. Rather, he closely observed what we naturally do anyway--or want to do--simplified it, then gave us a handle to do it at will.

So you already know this game and even already do it, if not yet as a "conscious discipline." So don't get your hopes up for new technology from another planet. This is something more down home, more familiar.

Okay, enough of the preamble. Let's roll one up and get it lit.

The Freedom Game: The *Discipline* of Joy.

The Freedom Game consists of four parts. I'll outline the parts here very quickly and then as the book unfolds we'll look deeper into how this basic game works in relation to the other games and what we might expect as we practice.

1. **The most loving thing we can do for ourselves and all those around us is to enjoy our lives.**

This is somewhat of a no-brainer, yes? Dr. Almayrac called it the **Law of Happiness**. (The way he stated it was, *"Enjoying my happiness is the most important thing for me and all those around me."*)

If we aren't enjoying our lives, then no matter what we are doing we are contributing to the worldwide woe. When we are at work, at school, at church, or at home, would it be best to be enjoying ourselves or not? And would we rather have a companion, co-worker, lover, friend who was enjoying himself, or herself, or one who wasn't?

It's an easy thing to say, to agree to in the moment: *The most loving (most important) thing we can do for ourselves and all those around us is to enjoy our lives.* With all the wars, the pollutions, corruptions, injustices and countless violent sadnesses ongoing in our world, to actually *live* our daily lives with such love, such joy, such happiness is somewhat revolutionary. (We'll get to that.) But don't we smoke pot simply because we want to enjoy ourselves? Enjoy our lives? Of course. Why else would we do it?

2. **We enjoy our lives when we enjoy the train of thought we are riding.**

Duh.

Dr. Almayrac calls this the Link because it links our happiness with the train of thought we are riding at any given moment. For example, we could be sitting on the beach in Hawaii, with the palm trees waving in the warm breeze and the blue ocean rolling onto the white sands, and still bum ourselves out by riding the train of thought: "*That stupid cabana boy didn't put an umbrella in my drink. That lazy bum, who does he think I am, blah blah blah. . . ."*

On the other hand, we could be stuck in Monday morning traffic with horns honking and gas fumes rising, but we have a big grin on our face, riding a train of thought, "*That was a sweet weekend, and maybe it portends many more, just like that. That type of weekend makes life worth living. . . . etc. etc."*

It's not *where* we are or *what* we're doing that "makes" us happy. It's what *train of thought* we're riding. (Thoughts do come in trains, yes? Sometimes it's only a single engine--a single thought that comes along. But most often, we all have *trains* of thought!)

It's what inner train we're riding, what we're holding in consciousness that determines whether or not we are enjoying ourselves, enjoying our lives, which is another way of saying whether or not we are loving ourselves. Again, this principle--*we enjoy our lives when we enjoy the train of thought we are riding*--is somewhat of a no-brainer, and easily tested. Is it possible to enjoy our lives while riding a train of thought we don't enjoy to ride?

Duh, no.

3. **Whenever necessary or appropriate, we simply ask, "*Do I enjoy riding this train of thought, yes or no?"* If the answer is not an immediate and spontaneous *yes*, it's a *no*.**

Here is where it gets "almost" too simple. And yet we have to be brave to ask this question: "**Am I enjoying riding this train of thought, yes or no**?" *If the answer is not an immediate and spontaneous yes, it's a no.*

This second part sets a very high and very obvious standard for our happiness. It's like when we ask our loved one, "*Do you love me?"* If there's a hesitation, ("*Well….*") we know we're in trouble. In the same way, when we ask ourselves whether we enjoy the train of thought we are riding, if the answer is, "*well . . .,*" we can assume that's a *no*.

If enjoying our lives really *is* the most loving thing we can do for ourselves and those around us ---- which I suggest it is--and if we enjoy our lives only when we enjoy our thought trains, **then it's not only useful but *necessary* to have a simple test** to tell us whether or not we actually *are* on the right train, the right path, actually are enjoying our lives. It's like, "is that a snake, or a stick?" We want to know right now, right here, without mistake.

Do I enjoy riding this train of thought, yes or no? If the answer's not an immediate and spontaneous *yes*, it's a *no*. This question is the simple test. The effect is like the binary processing going on in a computer. One of the things that makes binary processing so efficient is that there's never a question: it's either a 1 or a 0. The yes or no question is wonderfully efficient. *Do I enjoy riding this train of thought?* If it's not an immediate and spontaneous *yes*, it's a *no*. That's the high standard, so to speak. **It's a very efficient way of knowing whether we are getting high or bumming ourselves out.**

Generally, we don't need to use a test like this, or play a game or exercise like this when we are already enjoying ourselves. For example, let's say we're out bowling and we bowl a strike. We generally don't stop to ask, "*Do I enjoy this train of thought, yes or no*?" Of course we do. We don't even have to ask such a question.

But if we *should* stop to ask, and our answer is "yes," (I enjoy thinking that I just bowled a strike) that's perfect. Whenever the answer is "*yes, I enjoy this train of thought,*" we can safely keep riding whatever train of thought we happen to be riding. Life is good. We're feeling buzzed. On we go.

Most often, we will use this test, play the Freedom Game, in those areas and circumstances where we are *not* enjoying ourselves, e.g., when we are riding trains of thought we *don't* enjoy to ride. (As we all know, this can happen anywhere, even when we're bowling, or when we're water skiing or even when we're stoned!) So, that leads us to the action part of the Freedom Game:

4. If the answer is no, (I do not enjoy riding this particular train of thought) in order to maintain my high (my love, my joy) I have two options:

a. **Jump off the train of thought I don't enjoy to ride and find or create a train of thought I enjoy more;**
   or

b. **Choose to *enjoy* the train of thought that a moment before I was not enjoying.**

Performing option A is fairly obvious. If you don't enjoy a train of thought, then change it, just jump off, find a train of thought you enjoy more. Summed up in the popular East Coast phrase, *"fuhgaddaboudit."* Change the channel. Move on. Stop bumming yourself out with your own thoughts.

Option B is a little more subtle. One example I often give for Option B is: the boss calls you into the office and gives you a very short train of thought: "*You're fired*!' Upon first hearing it, you most likely don't enjoy that little train. (*Arrrgh! Uggh! Oh no! I'm fired!*)

That's the train most of us immediately start riding. Yet we are free to turn it around, decide to enjoy that little train. "*Yay! I'm fired! Finally! No more coming in, dealing with this s.o.b. I'm out! Fired! Thank God!"* The train of thought you didn't enjoy a moment before, the train that someone handed you . . . you now decide to enjoy. *It's your choice.*

Or your squabbling mate hands you another little train: *"I'm leaving."* At first, you don't enjoy that train of thought. And then . . . *hey, okay*! *Finally. It's about time. Let's quit this squabbling."* Again, your choice. We can choose to enjoy almost *any* train of thought.

"No [train of] thought is forbidden," Dr. Almayrac was fond of saying. We can enjoy almost *any* train!

So here's the Freedom Game, without comment. I encourage my clients to memorize it because it has taken over fifteen years to simplify this powerful life-game down to these few words. These particular words contain a few linguistic structures that make it more precise, more powerful, even though the general idea is simple.

I also encourage memorization simply because, when we're studying it, reading it, trying to memorize it, we can't help but to *start playing the game*!

The Freedom Game:

1. **The most loving thing I can do for myself and all those around me is to enjoy my life.**
2. **I enjoy my life when I enjoy the train of thought I am riding.**
3. **Whenever necessary, I ask, *Am I enjoying this train of thought, yes or no*. If the answer is not an immediate and spontaneous '*yes*,' it's a '*no*.'**
4. **If the answer is *yes*, that's perfect. I just keep riding the train of thought I'm riding. If the answer is *no*, then I have two options:**
   a. **Jump off the train of thought I don't enjoy to ride and find or create a train of thought I enjoy more; or**
   b. **Choose to *enjoy* the train of thought which a moment before I was not enjoying.**

Like smoking weed, this is not rocket science. And like I said, it took much more time to explain it here than it actually takes to do it. And **this isn't a game or process you can "test" just by reading, any more than smoking weed is something you can test by watching.**

You actually have to *try it, play the game,* see what it does for you! Naturally, I encourage you to use the Freedom Game while reading the rest of this book! Use it to tune in to your own joy. When I throw out some outrageous claim, (such as, *you are already always naturally happy*) you are free to ask yourself, *"Do I enjoy that train of thought, yes or no."* If it's not an immediate and spontaneous *yes*, it's a *no*.

In later chapters we'll explore in more detail some of the research on the nature of human consciousness and whether consciousness is at root *joyful,* as the yogis claim. When we personally experience the answer to this question (*is consciousness itself joyful*?) we will be much more confident that our joy is *always* at hand and will inevitably lead us to life's deeper truths.

True or Not True? That Is NOT the Question

At this point, however, let me simply point out that the question that we ask ourselves when playing with the Freedom Exercise is **not**, *"Is this train of thought true*?" That is not the question we are asking.

This whole "joyful" approach to our thinking process is somewhat subversive. (As is smoking pot, which may be one reason there are so many laws against it.) Contrary to cultural conditioning, if we want to put an end to both personal and communal suffering, we must begin with our own consciousness, and thus, with the trains of thought we are riding. The question as to whether the trains of thought we are currently riding are in fact *true* is, of course, an important question. But--*and here's where the subversion comes in*—whether our thoughts are true is not the *most* important question.

Truth, at least on the surface, so often seems to be a localized, culturally implanted "belief system". For example, in some cultures, it's true that a young widowed wife should throw herself on her deceased husband's funeral pyre. That's what's expected of her, because it's "true" that she's no longer valuable. That's what feels *true* in her culture.

Or in other cultures it's *true* that God/Allah wants young men or women to wrap dynamite around their waists and go into the market and blow themselves up to prove their faith and serve their people. This is what is offered as "true."

Other cultures--ours included--have less extreme "belief systems" that are put forth and accepted as "true." So the question, "Is this thought train I'm riding true" can lead us, so to speak, down some very wrong and violent tracks.

The question, "Do I enjoy riding this thought train" can take us beyond the cultural prejudices into deeper, more life-affirming territory. The widow does not actually enjoy the train of thought that would have her throw herself on the funeral pyre, nor does the young martyr enjoy the idea of suicide, though in each instance their cultures would have them ride such trains to their sad ends.

Thus, the question when playing the Freedom Game is not whether a thought train is true--it may or may not be. The game is simply whether or not we *enjoy* our momentary train of thought. *Do I enjoy riding this train of thought, yes or no?* If we don't enjoy a particular train of thoughts, we are *not* obliged to ride that train, think those thoughts, even if everybody around us says we must. (Thus begins the revolution, going beyond our cultural conditioning!)

As we'll discover in later chapters, our joy lies deeper than our daily mental machinations. Our joy will *always* take us to a deeper truth, and will *always* guide us to a more loving, more peaceable and authentic presence than if we continue following the mental monkey mind.

So whether a train of thought is true or not is *not* the question. The question is, simply, "*Do I <u>enjoy</u> riding this train of thought, yes or no*?"

With that somewhat hippie attitude, let's move to the next chapter where we take a first brief look at the pot high and the drug experience in general and see again why it is best not entered into as a competitive endeavor!

Chapter 3:

Rest in Peace, Timothy Leary:
Why Competition Can Be Deadly in the Drug World

"I like to keep a bottle of stimulant handy in case I see a snake, which I also keep handy.

---- W. C. Fields

I'm a nut on the Freedom Exercise. I play the game in my personal life, my family life, and my professional life. In my addictions counseling, the Freedom Game was always one of the first things I taught—shared--with new clients. Over the years I've seen the Freedom Game--or more precisely, the simple willingness to actually enjoy our lives by paying attention to what we're holding in consciousness--consistently and dramatically brighten people's lives. I love sharing such basic common sense.

My experience with this game over the last fifteen years or more confirms what Dr. Almayrac told me when he first shared it with me: **Nobody has ever reached the bottom of the joy lake**. The more we practice our joy, as a fundamental daily discipline, rather than as a hoped for future reward, the more joy we discover! And isn't joy what we're looking for when we get high?

Or is it?

It will be useful to come to some basic agreements here about our experiences with the ups and downs of the drug high, the ins and outs, giggles and frowns just to be certain we're on the same page. If our quest is the "*potless pot high*," we need to know what that high actually *is* so that we'll know when we experience it.

Competition Is *Not* Healthy

We might profit by sharing, and comparing our experiences with pot--and with drugs in general-- but right here from the start let's agree not to compete. One of the lessons I learned fairly early is that there was *always* going to be somebody who had taken more drugs than I -- a lot more. Even if I toked up every morning for twenty years, somebody else would have been buzzed morning *and* night, for thirty years. In the drug world there is always someone who has ingested larger dosages of a wider variety of drugs, over a longer period of time. And there will always be people who have much less experience.

I feel fortunate that after one particular harrowing experience I realized that these drug games were best *not* played in a competitive fashion. There are really no "champion" drug users nor are there amateurs, although sometimes these false *personas* do appear.

Our competitive culture is such that when most people are first introduced to the drug scene they go in with a certain amount of competitiveness already built into their personality. We all have at least a little desire to "keep up with the Joneses, or indeed, outdo the Joneses. In this particular arena, such conditioning can be literally deadly!

"Bet I can do more drugs than you can, Jones man."

"No way, dude, bet you can't."

"Yes, I can."

"No you can't."

"Yea? Watch this."

Kerplunk.

"Ok, ok. You win."

Turn On, Tune In...

In my own case, one night in the late 60's I went with a few of my college chums to hear the famed Harvard professor, Dr. Timothy Leary lecture in Boulder, Colorado on the history and future of the human condition. He was quite authoritative, (a Ph.D. teaching at Harvard!) inspirational (he made us laugh all night long) and offered what seemed like a bright, reasonable strategy for our lives, what with human history and the likely future being what it was, there in the late 60's. His impassioned conclusion was that we should all, "*turn on, tune in, drop out*." The way we do this, he suggested, was to smoke pot on the weekdays then take LSD on Sundays. Hmmm . . .

What he was suggesting, of course, was that we needed to *change the way we were thinking*, and thus the way we're acting and being on the planet. Undoing the obvious unhappiness throughout the world was a cause we could/should take up in our own lives, he said. We could only counter all the unhappiness in the world, he said, first by letting our own lives be more joyful. Pot and LSD were his recommended "High Ways".

Wasn't long, of course, before we realized that if we took LSD every Sunday, and smoked pot on weekdays, most of us weren't getting our brains mooshed back together in time for the next Sunday's melt down. Some of us realized that LSD every weekend might be a little much, though the daily pot seemed okay.

Others of us, of course, after first sampling the eclectic electric wonders of LSD, didn't want to wait for the weekend. LSD has a potential to take you to that place where time itself unravels. When conditioned thought is no longer in the way, it becomes quite clear that *every* day is a holiday--holy day. Seen from the peak of an LSD experience, it's obvious that *time* is only a way of thinking, a framework for thinking, and not a reality in itself. The difference between "Sunday time" and "Monday time" is a linguistic contrivance made up by humans.

More than one of my friends chose the "break-on-through" strategy--where LSD was (for a season) a daily—or every other day, every third day drug of choice. As far as I know, very few enjoy to keep that choice up for more than a few months (max), because LSD is simply not that kind of drug. Our brains do need to recharge, reformulate themselves. We simply can't live on the roller coaster, or on the loop de loop for any extended period of time.

But other drugs did indeed offer a daily maintenance type of high, a maintenance of happiness. And pot seemed--seems--to be the most benign of them all, more so than alcohol, and much more so than the various uppers or downers.

Drugs and alcohol basically change the way we are thinking--and change the way we are *feeling* about our thinking. In a nutshell, we enjoy the trains of thought we are riding more when we are stoned, or pleasantly buzzed, yes?

I was like most kids who were told how bad marijuana was and then, through personal experience, discovered that it was not so bad after all, at least not there in the short run. In fact, rather than being bad it seemed *good,* even *great.* It made my buddies and me giggle, sometimes even *roar* with laughter. (The thought trains we didn’t enjoy to ride before smoking we now enjoyed!)

Pot seemed to help us think about our lives, within and without, in a whole new light, with much more humor and compassion and with what seemed like brighter, wider, *higher* forms of thinking. “ What's so wrong with this?” we asked. Nothing, we quickly replied.

So we likewise wondered whether the *next* drug down the line might do something even better. If they were hiding the happy truth about pot, was there also something nice about hash, coke, or crack, ecstasy, meth, mushrooms, LSD, barbiturates, heroin, whatever? Let's find out.

And we found that the other drug highs were different from pot, yet the immediate changes in thinking and feeling were just as obvious, just as real, most often pleasurable and generally came with only slightly objectionable side effects. So many of us started looking for the exact right combination to see if we could stay high, stay righteous, stay feeling fine all the time. (Welcome to life on earth!)

As I said, I feel fortunate that I realized early in the game the limitations of this new journey we were on. Although I was along for the ride—sometimes I was even driving the bus--I (mostly) wasn't in competition with my fellow voyagers. Some of those on that oval track ahead of us in this race to test how many drugs we could explore --- or more precisely, how good we could feel, sustained over how long a period--seemingly winning this race, suddenly fell over dead, or were picked up and thrown in the slammer for extended periods of time, or ended up in the loony bin. Such observations slowed me down. I realized I didn't need to race so fast, didn't need to keep up with the Joneses. It was a healthy lesson to learn. Sooner or later most people experimenting with feeling good through various drugs learn this same lesson. Some folks, of course, don't.

The Basics of the Drug High

Here's the key: it's not the *drug* that we're after. It's the *feel good*. To arrive at the *feel good*, the drug changes our thinking, and how we're *feeling* about our thinking. (The classic description of morphine: *"The pain's still there. You just don't care."*)

Folks who get attracted to the experience *enjoy* the way the drug changes their thinking. For the folks who don't get caught, it's simply because they don't enjoy the way the drug changes their thinking. Duh.

Here's the catch: The drug—be it pot or smack or somewhere in between--does not *guarantee* enjoyable thinking! Indeed, **as human beings we are endowed with an innate freedom and power and inclination to think *anything* we want, in any way we want, regardless of the present influence of drugs—or friends or family or political affiliation--on our thinking**. Drugs, and friends and family can have a big influence on our thinking, especially in the short run, but they are not the final arbiter of our thinking. Thus, due to our mostly conditioned thinking, we can and often do bum ourselves out--- or let someone else bum us out--simply by hopping on a train of thoughts we don't enjoy to ride, whether we're stoned or not.

(*"We enjoy our happiness when we enjoy the train of thoughts we are riding."*)

So in this book when we talk about and compare drug experiences we can observe from the first that it's *not* a straight track we're running on, or even a nice oval, though the metaphor of running a race toward happiness may be useful. The lanes go every which way. The finish line for Jane may come yards, or years before the finish line for Sally, just as the starting lines for this "race to joy" are all over the field. And where Johnny is doing a sprint, Billy may be in a marathon. Where Cosmo is doing low hurdles, Griz is doing the pole vault. Where Rene is running in the heat of summer, Lucille is in the cold. Everybody's inner experience is different, and valid, simply because it's their own.

In the same way, if we can agree that drug use—the drug experience, and the pot high in particular--- is not a competitive endeavor, then likewise, **the potless pot high need not be a competitive quest**. In our drug experiences it's not about what we have ingested, or how much or for how long that is important. What's important is what we've learned about how to most directly, most consistently, access our own joy, our own natural being, our original being.

The Freedom Exercise suggests that accessing our joy is the most loving and most practical thing we can do for ourselves and everybody else. Contrary to what mainstream culture teaches and many "drug rehab" specialists have been trained to think, our own inner joy truly is a trustworthy navigational beacon. The surprise is that this joy is always there--- drug or no drug--- because joy is a native quality of our being, a quality of consciousness itself. This is a nice thing to discover, a fundamental lesson to learn.

So for the rest of this book, when we compare our get-high experiences, and discuss the various games that make up the potless pot high, it will be easier if we drop the "one-up" approach, the deadly competition, and simply observe that we are fellow voyagers, not in a contest with each other.

"Authority" in these matters is not determined by how many drugs we've taken, or not taken, over how long a period, or the exercises and meditations we've engaged in (or who's writing the book and who's reading!)

Rather, lets give authority to the joy we're experiencing and sharing *today*; let's give authority to the tricks we've picked up along the way that allow each of us individually to experience love, peace, and joy in our daily walk around world.

In this book let's just relax and enjoy each other's history, and company, and see what we might learn next, where we might go . . .

This Potless Pot High is easy so far, yes?

Good news: It gets even easier.

Chapter 4:

All You Need Is Love, (and a Quick Little Toke): 90 Million Pot Highs = 90 Million Lovers

Professional Get High Guy

As briefly mentioned, my own destiny led me to also experience the other side of drug use and abuse-- where I found myself in a helping mode. Here's how it happened:

At the height of the Vietnam War, I was drafted, but refused induction into the armed services. (I'd refuse again, a thousand times!) I didn't run away, didn't "dodge" the consequences of refusing the draft. I showed up at the Federal Court House on my draft date, then refused to step forward. ("Make love, not war!") I was convicted the following year, when I was teaching high school in a high poverty district in San Antonio, Texas, and sentenced to work two years in "community service" in lieu of military service. It was up to me to find-- or invent-- the community service that I was to perform. (Curiously, "teaching" in a high poverty high school didn't qualify as a community service!)

To make a long story short, I founded and directed a drug education and treatment center because, as a young man, drugs was what I knew, and where my curiosity and passion were, and what my 60's generation was exploring.

For the next nine years I worked helping street people and returning Vietnam Vets and housewives in their homes deal with out-of-control drug problems. I also developed drug education programs for grade school, junior high, high school and college classrooms. My foundation evolved to eventually provide medical, legal and psychological counseling to hard core drug addicts, as well as for occasional users, and educational services to community agencies and public schools.

During these years working in drug education and treatment I received training and was supervised by a series of medical professionals, psychiatrists and psychologists including representatives of the Menninger Clinic, the Haight-Ashbury Free Clinic, the National Free Clinic Association, the U.S. Department of Health, Education and Welfare, the U.S. Department of Probation and Parole, and other professional agencies. The treatment models I was exposed to during this time included Gestalt, Skinnerian, Adlerian, Jungian and other offshoots of contemporary addiction treatment theories, as well as much face time with the Mother Ship of addictions in our time: the 12 step programs.

In the last five years of my work in drug education and treatment I had the additional specific job description of exploring "alternative approaches" to attaining the euphoric states of consciousness sought after through drug use. In this capacity I had a wide exposure to both contemporary and traditional schools of meditation and psychic exploration, including bio-feedback, hatha yoga, transcendental meditation, Taoist alchemy, tantric Buddhism, "pure land" Buddhism, Zen Buddhism (*yikes!*) Siddha Yoga, the Kabbala, Christian esoteric mysticism and Sufi paradigms, among others.

It might be interesting to note that throughout my years of conducting intense drug education, treatment and "alternatives" research, I still occasionally smoked pot, in private and socially (as did 80% of all other "drug treatment" specialists). This was--and in many places still is--no more exceptional for me and my generation (as with the generations that followed) than is having a beer after work, or a glass of wine with dinner. Just as a beer or a glass of wine after work can be easy and natural, or can lead to a lifetime of problems, so too can pot use.

The simple point I'm making here is that I feel quite familiar with drug use, and abuse, and with the treatment and failure of treatment. I recognize that many others may have more familiarity, with both drugs and drug treatments, while others have less. Fortunately, I'm at a stage in my life where I most often (though not always) chuckle at and feel great compassion for the craziness and social drama surrounding the drug experience. I am not frightened by it. Or offended by it. I feel compassion and curiosity rather than condemnation, competition or antagonism when people share their different drug experiences, including "rehab." (Because of my long-time work with tobacco addictions, people share their different drug experiences with me all the time!)

I share my background here so that when I suggest that I really have, after all these years, found a way to experience a natural, potless pot high, a weedless enlightenment, I'm not just blowing smoke, (pun intended). I've got years of comparative data, with both personal and professional experience upon which to stake such a claim.

So again, if our quest is for a potless pot high, what exactly does this high look like, feel like? In Chapters Six and Seven we'll delve into the laboratory research and neuro-physiological effects of marijuana --- what happens to the brain waves, the heartbeat, the anatomic and metabolic functions--to make sure that the potless pot high, our "replacement high", actually does mirror the best, most benign of these effects. For now, let's look at it from the layman's point of view.

100 Million Different Pot Highs, 100 Million Lovers

With at least 100 million Americans having tried pot (and around the world the number climbs close to a billion) we can assume that there might be 100 million different "weed fueled enlightenments", 100 million different "pot highs". Since everyone is different, we're each going to experience pot in a different way. Still, it will help if we can agree on the *general* nature of the pot high.

Here's the challenge: trying to describe the experience of the pot high is a little bit like trying to describe the experience of falling in love. We can assume that the experience of falling in love will be different for each of us and that it will be somewhat different for men than it is for women, somewhat different for old people than for young people, different for the farmer than for the disco-dancer, different for the scholar than for the sit-com watcher.

At root, however, falling in love means we now have something we enjoy to think—a person we enjoy to think about, and a future and maybe an immediate past that we enjoy to think about. The inner lights in our thinking process--- and thus our feeling process-- have been turned on.

Same holds true for pot. The inner lights come on—we suddenly find something we enjoy to think about, or we enjoy thinking about the old things in new ways. Just as our individual time and place, and our personal, familial and social background make the experience of falling in love unique for each of us, the same is true with getting high, yet the underlying mental qualities are similar.

For almost everyone, when we first fall in love or get high, we experience a change for the better in our immediate mood--we feel happier than we did before, and the whole world seems bright and full of wonderful things, new possibilities. When we fall in love these feelings generally come about over a period of days or weeks or months. With pot, these feelings arise immediately, within minutes.

When we fall in love, or get high, it often happens that what was interesting to us before is perhaps not so interesting now. But what didn't hold our attention for more than a moment before now might hold our attention completely. Many of the things that made us angry or uptight before we got high, (or fell in love) now don't faze us. But things that previously didn't bother might now drive us bonkers.

Our thoughts change. Our moods change. *Even our tastes in music change*! And we don't feel so alone, or at odds, when we're in love, or feeling high.

And where we were lethargic before we fell in love or got high, we now have energy. Or visa versa: Where before we had been running around like the mad hatter, we now relax, take things as they come, enjoy the moment's scenery.

Both getting high and falling in love involve subtle and not so subtle changes in thinking and feeling, such that the world seems brighter, softer, more welcoming, less threatening than it did before. This softening, brightening, relaxing effect in our mental chambers is what makes the drug high so attractive. And although the "real world" might tell us it's not right-- we should not fall in love with that particular person, or at this particular time, or in this particular situation, or that we should not get high like we do, it's just not right--**our immediate, first-hand experience tells us otherwise**. Most of us are generally quite ready to go against what the "real world" tells us we *should* do in exchange for this new-found joy-- be it our new lover or our new high!

Most experienced pot users say they can feel the effects after even one or two "tokes," or inhales. To bring about the feelings of "new love" in such a quick and efficient manner--even though it's illegal in most places-- is naturally quite attractive to a very large segment of people.

What Other Metaphors?

I don't feel I'm over-glamorizing the pot high here. For those who might feel offended by the comparison between getting high and first falling in love, the question arises as to what other comparison might be made? Yes, getting stoned can be a little bit like riding the roller coaster, which is fun. But you don't want to ride it two or three times a day, or even two or three times a week! And certainly not to relax after work. There's something softer, gentler, more immediate that is happening here than just a roller coaster ride.

And yes, getting stoned can be like attending a far-out, Technicolor 3-D sci-fi movie. Such an escape can be fun, relaxing. Yet again, would we want to start or end our day, every day, by going to the movies? There's something more "real" about getting stoned than "escapism."

Getting high may at times be akin to glimpsing, or even visiting the vast chasms of infinite space. Such experiences can be very beautiful, even profound and certainly exciting. But we generally don't need to make such visits, or enjoy such visits more than once or twice every so often.

The point here is that the pot high is much easier, more benign, more comfortable, more *personal* than what the mainstream media and the *Just Say No* folks would suggest. Again, the attraction of pot is that it most often (but not always) offers an immediate feeling of love, of joy and ease.

So, we can understand how the pot high is so attractive. Especially for young males--who seem, according to most surveys, slightly more attracted to pot than do females---this "socially acceptable" way (in some social circles) to feel and express love, happiness or ease is a welcome change. The pot high is especially attractive to those who are young, unattached, and perhaps feeling a bit estranged from family, friends and social institutions-- (the profile of "at risk" youth!). Wouldn't it make sense that this "falling in love" type of experience would quickly gain their devotion? Especially if all—or even some--of their friends are likewise "falling in love" in this easy manner.

In general, people don't want to become more jangled, more shook up, more alienated than they already are. If that's all the drug experience offered—which, again, is what the above ground propaganda, legal authorities and many rehab "experts" would lead us to believe--there would be no long-term attraction to drug use. But "jangled, shook up, alienated" is *not* the experience of the drug high, at least not immediately, not in the short run, though after-effects can indeed be so. The high itself is much more like falling in love, being happy with the world and the day.

This is just one journeyman's description of what pot has to offer: an immediate, generally reliable experience of falling in love, (e.g., a feeling of "oneness,"to a greater or lesser degree). With such a description it can be seen why the war against pot is thus somewhat akin to a war against falling in love! From the beginning, that's a losing war!

Back to the first two principles of The Freedom Game:

1. *The most loving thing we can do for ourselves and all those around us is to enjoy our lives.*

2.*We enjoy our lives when we enjoy the thought train we are riding.*

On the surface, these principles don't seem have a thing to do with drugs. And yet . . .

Ok, yes, of course, there are differences, major differences between smoking pot and falling in love. We can take the metaphor only so far. Falling in love is something that blossoms and gets better over weeks and months and years. Getting high happens much quicker, but doesn't necessarily unfold as much. Falling in love generally leads one to grow ever more beautiful, ever stronger and more at peace with one's self and the world. Getting high, we're generally not that lucky.

More specifically, when we fall in love we are engaged with another person--we give energy, attention and consideration to another person. And then this generally opens the door to giving such attentive energy to still more people--to children, and parents, and brothers and sisters of the loved one.

Or maybe we fall in love with a particular field of interest--bonsai, say, or molecular biology or pecan growing, knitting or oil painting. We've found something we enjoy to think about, and it gets better and better the deeper we get into it. Here again our love leads us into ever broader experiences of our field--- and to the people and places and events occurring in that field.

But the experience of "falling in love" which pot allows does not necessarily involve other people, or even other fields of interest. Indeed, over time, the pothead realizes that other people are not really necessary for this "falling in love" experience. The pothead tends to become more and more disassociated. In fact, the pot high tends, over time, to lead to falling in love *with one's self!*

At first, of course, this can be healthy, and right, especially if there has been a sense of "un-love" or no love or muted love in the person's experience. Pot can warm such a person up, make him or her feel alive again, whole and happy. This is healthy, fruitful.

But the experience of love that the pot high offers can also lead to self-absorption, loneliness and alienation. (Again, I'm not condemning here. I'm merely relating my own personal experience and the experience of friends and clients.) It can be unhealthy, unfruitful.

In My Room, In My Room

I'm pointing here now to what often happens with long-term, daily pot use. Persistent long-term use does not *inevitably* lead down this path. I've known and loved many pot heads who, after many years, still have quite healthy, vibrant, outgoing relationships with lots of people--their family, their friends, their community. And they do so with a depth, sensitivity and compassion previously not expressed.

In general, however, pot use does not lead to such outgoing relationships. After all, if you can be "in love" in your room, by yourself, or with your best friend, or lover, why go to the hassle of going out? The Beach Boys' Brian Wilson, with the help of Gary Usher, wrote a powerful song (*"In My Room"*) expressing this exact phenomenon, based on his own experience. Here are some of the lyrics:

There's a world where I can go

And tell my secrets to

In my room . . .

In this world I lock out
All my worries and my fears
. . .Do my dreaming and my scheming
lie awake and pray
Do my crying and my sighing laugh at yesterday

Now it's dark and I'm alone
But I won't be afraid
In my room

For some people, especially young folks, when they first discover the joys of pot, their frequency of use can increase dramatically. Rather than being just an occasional indulgence, this "lovely" loving experience captures their attention. Then, rather than imbibing just once a month or once every couple of weekends, it becomes a two or three or four times a week thing, and then every day. (How often do *you* want to be with your new lover?)

Many of these folks, when they find themselves so enamored with pot that they are suddenly doing it every day, or every other day, and they see their other social involvements and responsibilities falling away, get a little worried, or frightened. Their social conscience kicks in--along with maybe their pocketbook concerns and awareness of the legal and social risk.

So most people--especially people who already have much love and productive activity in their lives—naturally, intentionally back off. They determine not to smoke so much. So they don't. It can be that simple. No problem.

For many people, smoking pot happens only occasionally, once or twice every month or two, or once or twice every six months. With these folks, pot smoking is again no problem, no big deal.

Of course, many individuals try pot once or twice or three times, find it makes them sick or dizzy or out of control, and they simply don't enjoy such an experience.

They don't like what it does to their thinking. Or maybe they find it does nothing at all to their thinking. So they partake lightly, or not at all when pot is offered at social events. For these people, the "love bug"--the love experience from pot--simply never happened. They get on with their lives--find love, joy, happiness in career, family, sports (alcohol, sex, church, whatever . . .). Again, so be it.

But a certain percentage of people in our society feel that smoking pot-- falling in love this way--is a right, natural and even holy thing to do. Many of the 100 million who have tried pot feel both justified and motivated to smoke pot whenever they damn well please--once or twice a day, two or three or four times a day, or a week, or a month.

(Although, as most pot smokers will quickly attest, *all* marijuana use might be classified as "medicinal," we're not talking here about those who use marijuana for specific medicinal purposes. That's a whole different story—and a whole different book, though in later chapters we will look briefly at the health benefits of both pot and the Potless Pot High Games.)

The Average Pot Head

Many average, every-day pot smokers—especially in their early years--don't necessarily try to put the brakes on their pot use. They have moved beyond--or laid to rest--the social conscience which argues against it. They have determined that long term pot use is an easy, enjoyable, mostly benign indulgence and that whatever drawbacks such regular use might create, such drawbacks are small compared to the benefits. They may be right.

When we compare someone's regular pot use to all the other problems in the world--the hunger, the political corruption, human slavery, wars, the daily despair of many crack and heroine addicts, the unfolding debilitation of alcoholism, the violent effects of raw political or economic ambition—then regular pot use does indeed appear to be a very minor problem, or no problem at all. In comparison to other "sins" of the contemporary world, a regular pot high--a regular falling in love---doesn't seem half bad! Indeed, it seems more than half good!

(Again, we are not discussing here the medicinal use of marijuana. Many people find daily use of marijuana a medical necessity--to combat physical pain or nausea or other complications of injury or disease. To deny these people relief because of political and cultural superstition is, in my view, criminal. We'll talk more about this in Chapter 16.)

Whether you are a long-term pot-head, or whether you are an occasional user, or a "once-was-enough" person, here's the good news: when you begin to consciously practice *The Potless Pot High* games, beginning with the Freedom Game, you'll discover you get high (fall in love) and stay high (stay in love) and keep getting higher (let your love grow deeper) without brakes. And you'll find yourself "in love" while you're still taking care of your daily business – indeed, taking better care than you have ever done before. And your outer social life will be more vibrant, more rewarding than it has ever been, and yet you'll find yourself still regularly distracted, like pot heads are wont to do, with a lady bug on a leaf, or the beauty of a sunset, or the innocent grace of a child skipping rope.

Promises, promises. Enough head talk. It's time to take another hit. Let's move on to the second game in the *Potless Pot High*: The Peace Game.

Chapter Five:

Game Two: The Peace Practice

What High Works Best While Visiting the Nursing Home?

If you get down and quarrel every day,
you're saying prayers to the devil, I say
--- Bob Marley

As mentioned, I'm a nut on the Freedom Game. I play with it every day (*Do I enjoy riding this thought train, yes or no?*) I share it with friends and clients. I'm secretly addicted to it. It keeps me buzzed, grinning.

And it keeps others buzzed, too. When my book, *The Enlightened Smoker's Guide to Quitting* first came out it was distributed by Penguin in the United States, Canada, Great Britain, Australia, New Zealand and South Africa, so I received many reports from around the world about the power of joy for overcoming all manner of afflictions. This is why in my addictions practice I always begin a new relationship by first sharing the Freedom Game. If we're not following our joy, what are we following?

One afternoon I was sharing the Freedom Game with a new client, "Denise." Besides her addiction to smoking,

Denise was burdened with a number of other problems, including a serious shoulder injury for which she needed surgery (and the doctor would not operate until she quit smoking) along with a lifelong struggle with depression. Denise had seasons in her life when she was so overcome with depression that she was not able to get out of bed for weeks at a time.

In our first session, after getting to know each other a little, I shared the Freedom Game with her, affirming that enjoying her happiness was the most loving and most practical thing she could do for herself and those around her. I took her through the four steps, and then, after my presentation, handed her a little green card on which I have printed the Freedom Game. (I give these "Freedom Game" green cards out to everybody!)

Denise took the card, looked at it, looked at me, looked back at the card and then with a deep sigh set it back on my desk.

"Bullshit", she said.

I laughed. I appreciated her candor. She said out loud what I knew others had secretly thought.

For most of her life people had been telling Denise that she should just "be happy." Don't think about it. Cheer up. *Blah blah blah*. And here was one more counselor telling her the same thing. She wasn't buying it.

I stuck by my guns.

"There's something in you," I suggested, "that is your power, your guide. I call it your joy, but I'm not addicted to the word. We can use whatever word you want."

We talked some more, and it was clear that Denise had no interest in using any spiritual terms. Didn't want to call it soul, or spirit, atman or Tao, certainly not the "Christ mind." She was very alienated from that whole sphere. After talking for a while I suggested the word *peace*.

"Well yes, I could sure use more peace in my life," she said.

"That's it, then", I said. "Let's use that".

Our relationship turned out very nice. Denise did quit smoking, had a successful surgery and was "on the mend" in the other areas of her life. Still, it was clear to me that what Denise said out loud about the seeming simplicity, and perhaps naiveté of the Freedom Game (*bullshit!*) others were also thinking, though more politely to themselves.

Even my wife, loving companion of a 100 years or so, when talking about the Freedom Game, once said, "I know it's true. I just wish it didn't sound so corny."

So now, thanks to Denise (and my wife) in addition to the green card I also, at some point, give out a blue card that has The Peace Game on it. Here it is:

The Peace Game:

1. The most generous thing we can do for ourselves and all those around us, in every circumstance and every relationship is to practice peace of mind.

2. We practice peace of mind when we are at peace with the thought train we are riding, the stories we are telling ourselves and others.

3. Whenever necessary or appropriate, we ask, "*Am I at peace riding this thought train, telling these stories, yes or no*?" If the answer is not an immediate and spontaneous *yes*, it's a *no*.

4. If the answer is *yes* (I'm at peace with this thought train, these stories), perfect. We're practicing our peace. If the answer is *no* (I'm not at peace riding this thought train, or telling these stories) then in order to return to peace I have two options:

a. Jump off the thought train I'm riding or stop telling the stories with which I am not at peace and find or

create thought trains or stories with which I am more at ease; or

b. Choose to be at peace with the thought trains and or stories that a moment before were troubling me.

When we are at peace with our own thought trains and stories, we are at peace and bring peace to the world.

Again, as easy as lighting a bowl, yes?

The Same but Different: Peace in the Nursing Home

Sometimes, "*enjoying*" our thought trains seems to be asking a bit much. Sometimes peace, rather than joy, is the best we can muster. And likewise, the pot high is often not so much a matter of laughing, giggling, slapping our knee and enjoying ourselves as it is a matter of simply releasing our un-ease, releasing the unconscious tension of everyday life, *i.e.,* finding a little peace. (It's not a coincidence that the "peace movement" has so many pot heads! It's a direct experience: peace is better than strife!)

During the season when I first began sharing the peace practice with people, my old mama was in the nursing home, making her transition to the other world, but slowly, slowly, over a number of years. Anyone who has been to a nursing home knows that it's an environment that is a challenge to our joy. If we go in feeling up, bright and cheery, unless we work very consciously to keep such a mood, it's generally not long before the images, sounds, smells and general mood of the place start to work on us. We can come out of the nursing home a bit dazed, worse for wear.

It was my destiny to be the one in the family to visit our mother and manage her care on a regular basis. (One of my siblings was out of state, the other was out of country.) As was my habit in other areas of my life, when I went to the nursing home I would endeavor to play the Freedom Game--*do I enjoy this thought I'm riding, yes or no*? And then I would see the old folks sitting in wheel chairs with their chins on their chests. Hear cries for help down the corridor. And then into my old mama's room. She was bedridden and highly medicated, with a roommate who was not all there. *Do I enjoy this thought train, yes or no?*

No, of course not.

And yet, could I be *at peace* with the circumstance? Did I need to automatically resist, recoil, moan and bemoan the circumstance, either outwardly or inwardly? Would that help me or my old mama or anyone else there? Of course not.

In the nursing home, I found the Peace Game to be much more applicable, and *do-able*, than was the Freedom Game. As it is with so many other people who had led full and vibrant lives, the nursing home became my mother's final "waiting station." I could wish it otherwise but this was the reality--- her reality and mine.

So, in the months and years while she was stationed there, I regularly spent much time in the "waiting station" with my mom. I'm happy to say that we also shared a calm, ever deepening peace in her last days, weeks and months. Could we ask for it to be different?

Away from Pain, Towards More Pleasure

Motivational experts suggest that we have two basic drives: one is *away* from pain, the other is *toward* more pleasure. Obviously, pot helps us to fulfill both these motivations---away from pain, towards more pleasure--sometimes efficiently, sometimes not so efficiently.

My experience with the Peace and Freedom games---these simple games we play with the trains of thought running through our own inner station-- is that they likewise help us do exactly that: move away from (release) the turmoil, the tension and chaos so prevalent in our lives today (*am I at peace with this train of thought, yes or no?)* and access the simple, uncomplicated joy that we knew as children (*do I enjoy this train of thought, yes or no?*).

So now we have the first two games of the Potless Pot High. My own experience with these games can be compared to one's experience with the game of golf. We learn the basics quite easily: *Take a club--any club you want--and hit that white ball, and then keep hitting it until you hit it into the hole.*

In the same way, "***Pay attention to the trains of thought that are going through your station and if you don't enjoy a train of thought or are not at peace with a train of thought, either jump off that train or decide to enjoy it, or at least be at peace with it.***"

It's obvious we can summarize these first two games in a sentence, as I just did. However, as with golf, to master these games takes a little more practice, a practice that can lead to a lifetime of ever-deepening pleasure and insight.

Speaking of a lifetime of ever-deepening pleasure and insight, isn't that exactly what we were trying to attain, and to one degree or another actually *did* attain (for a while) with our regular or irregular imbibing of the herb? In the next chapter we'll look at some of the research behind the neuro-physiological effects of cannabis use, and see if these first two games The Freedom Game and The Peace Practice might indeed take us to the same place. After all, as we can agree, "ever-deepening pleasure and insight" is an attractive proposition, and a worthy quest, even if the boss or the mother-in-law is not yet on board.

Chapter 6:

Your Brain on Drugs:

Enjoying Alpha, Beta, Theta, Delta and Those Sweet, Sweet Gamma Waves

"The highest, most varied and lasting pleasures are those of the mind." -- Arthur Schopenhauer

The next several chapters explore what happens to our brains after toking up. Knowing what's happening in there--understanding the neuro-biological mechanics of the "get high" experience-- allows us to do it more intentionally, more consciously, if we want, and thus allows us to get higher and stay higher longer (with or without the herb!)

Knowing what's happening in there, we'll know better how to drive and steer the space ship. Without such an understanding, it's hit or miss.

To state the obvious: smoking weed changes our inner mental experience. More specifically, it changes our brain waves, and the place from which those waves are emanating. Effecting such change is why we do it. (Or used to do it.) If weed didn't change things in there, move things around, we wouldn't smoke it. And because it *does* change things inside, is why some folks don't like it. Whether we like it or not, pot *does* change our brain waves, changes our mind. And just as obviously, the Potless Pot High games, if they are to mimic the get high experience, must also change the brain waves.

Is Getting High a Biological Urge?

In order to better understand the changes in our brain after toking up, let's first look quickly at what's going on in the brain right *before* we get stoned. In our normal, everyday state of consciousness, why on earth would we agree to change the inner structures? Why are we willing, even *attracted* to change our brain waves in this way? What are we up to? What are we looking for? Why do we do it?

Many in the "recovery" business suggest that getting high is a mostly selfish effort to "escape reality"—or escape a bad childhood, or unhappy environment, or faulty self–image. (In response to such analysis, the 60's icon Wavy Gravy neatly responded, "Only the jailers are against escape.")

A more compassionate interpretation is offered by the Buddhists who suggest we engage in such behavior in our honest attempt to "end the suffering," and more particularly, our psychological suffering, even if it's just the suffering of a boring, uneventful "same ol' same ol'" day hanging out in the modern rat race. Perhaps.

On a more upbeat note, Andrew Weil, M.D., one of the brightest lights of contemporary healing, the kindly guru of multi-disciplinary "well-being," suggests that getting high—or more specifically, changing our consciousness--is a *biological* urge, common to all people in all cultures at all times. (Don't we quickly, spontaneously *enjoy* that thought trains more than the previous ones?)

> "It is my belief," Dr. Weil wrote, "that the desire to alter consciousness periodically is an innate, normal drive analogous to hunger or the sexual drive. Note that I do not say 'desire to alter consciousness by means of chemical agents.' Drugs are merely one means of satisfying this drive; there are many

> others… In postulating an inborn drive of this sort, I am not advancing a proposition to be proved or disproved, but simply a model to be tried out for usefulness in simplifying our understanding of our observations. The model I propose is consistent with observable evidence. In particular, the omnipresence of the phenomenon argues that we are dealing not with something socially or culturally based, but rather with a biological characteristic of the species. Furthermore, the need for periods of non-ordinary consciousness begins to be expressed at ages far too young for it to have much to do with social conditioning. Anyone who watches very young children, without revealing his presence, will find them regularly practicing techniques that induce striking changes in mental states. Three- and four-year-olds, for example, commonly whirl themselves into vertiginous stupors. They hyperventilate and have other children squeeze them around the chest until they faint. They also choke each other to produce loss of consciousness."

Following Dr. Weil's observations, it seems possible that what we are doing--what the brain is doing--both when we are getting high and when we are looking for alternative ways of getting high, is responding to a deep *biological urge!*

We may even intuit that the brain itself, pursuing its own highest expression (so to speak) wants to--needs to--periodically change its "ordinary" frequencies, **change what train it's riding**! This goes far in helping to explain why sports, even just watching sports, is so popular. Win or lose, over the course of a game, brain waves change again and again: high, low, quiet, fast, tension, release. When there is a "rout," when one team or player is clearly going to win and the competition is low, we lose interest simply because the brain is not being given opportunity to "change brain wave frequency."

The same phenomenon--rapidly changing our brain wave frequencies--can occur when watching a good movie, or taking a walk or going to a party with new people.

Changing our brain waves is a very natural, very common "attraction" or event. Such changes can be a sign of a healthy psyche! (Folks in the nursing home often don't want their brain waves changed!)

Which takes us neatly to the question--- what exactly are these "brain wave frequencies" that we're talking about? Are they measurable?

Brain Wave Frequencies

Neuro-scientists measure and categorize brain waves according to how fast they vibrate--their frequency (measured in Hertz)--and give different names to the different brain wave frequencies. Researchers don't always agree as to exactly where (on the Hertz scale) one state starts and another ends, although there is general agreement as to the unique effects associated with each state.

When it comes to brain waves, much is yet to be learned. For example, "faster" does not always mean better, easier, more intelligent or more enjoyable (though sometimes it does). "Slower" does not necessarily mean less intelligent or less powerful, though it may. A sparrow beats its wings much faster than an eagle. Is there more intelligence, more power expressed in a sparrow than an eagle? Hmm . . . In other words, frequency is not all there is to it.

Most researchers suggest that humans have four primary brain wave states: Beta, Alpha, Theta, and Delta, and most will agree to a fifth: Gamma. Here's a quick simplified description (with a tip of the hat to Mark Vandekeere, for his eloquent summary, and to Ann Wise, for her "awakened mind" approach to brainwaves):

BETA waves (13-30+ Hz.) These are our daily "walk around" brain waves--what we emit when we're doing the laundry, going to work, painting the house, doing the taxes. The "beta state" is mostly associated with outward directed attention, when we are engaged in normal 3-D activity, perceiving and evaluating outer forms and data through the senses. Beta is also dominant when we are fearful, angry, worried, hungry or surprised. Studying this chapter, analyzing brain waves would normally rely on "beta" activity.

ALPHA waves. (8 to 13 Hz). People who meditate, and therapists and researchers who use bio-feedback often talk about going into an "alpha state." This state is associated with an alert, non-drowsy but nevertheless relaxed, tranquil state of awareness. In alpha we are aware of, but not so engaged or driven by, or aroused by, the 3-D world. In the alpha state we've stepped back a bit, into a pleasant inward awareness. We have a higher sense of the integral unity between body, mind and the world at large. We're present, attentive, but relaxed, quietly enjoying ourselves and the world we're in. (We used to assume that getting stoned was simply a matter of moving from the beta state into the alpha state. That's part of it, but not the whole enchilada). A fitting contemporary image of the alpha state is the television commercial showing the couple lounging in side-by-side bathtubs, overlooking the sea as the sun is setting (with the culturally approved drug of choice---cocktails---- waiting on the side table.)

THETA waves (4 to 8 Hz). We produce theta waves most often during our "REM" states of sleeping. REM is short for "rapid eye movement", which researchers have documented is most often present when we are dreaming. However, although Theta is associated with the dreaming state we do occasionally experience the theta state while we are awake, when meditating, daydreaming or intentionally slowing our brain activity. Some folks have trained themselves to consciously move into the theta state to accomplish particular "inner work" such as future visioning or to gain deeper insight into projects or problems. The theta state is often associated with increased recall, creativity, imagery and visualization; it is the door to the subconscious, if not the subconscious itself. Some have referred to the theta state as "*thinkerless thinking*," where thought is free-flowing, impersonal. For most of us, "waking theta" is what we briefly experience right before falling asleep.

DELTA waves (.5 to 4 Hz). These very slow brain waves are generally associated with deep dreamless sleep or, sometimes, a deep trance. Delta is associated with bodily self-healing, rest and rejuvenation. Some researchers have found that when delta is dominant there is an increased release of growth hormone from the pituitary gland. For most of us, delta is dominant only during deep levels of non-REM sleep. When we awaken feeling as though we "slept well," it's generally because we spent a lot of time in the delta state, repairing and rejuvenating. Again, researchers have found that some meditators, yogis or trained bio-feedback practitioners are able to go into a delta state at will. (Since Delta is associated with mental and physical rest, healing and rejuvenation, this is a very useful talent to nourish!)

GAMMA waves (30+ Hz.) Gamma waves are those relatively rare, generally short-lived, very rapid brain waves measured above Beta--from 30Hz up to a hundred or more. Gamma waves are associated with "peak experiences"---visions, insights, intense emotional, psychic or spiritual "breakthroughs," as well as with "breakdowns," again on various levels. Often in the gamma state we suddenly see the big picture; we learn large chunks about the world or about ourselves in a single instant. Where once the Native Americans went on a "Vision Quest," many now go on a "Gamma Quest." Six of one, half dozen of the other, some (physicists) would say. Some folks diagnosed with bi-polar disorder experience, in their manic phases, extended periods of gamma waves with seemingly heightened intelligence.

It would be nice if we could explain everything--including what it means to get stoned, or to fall in love--simply by describing the brain wave activity, moving from one state, one frequency, to another. (Some biologists and geneticists suggest we can.) Yes, stoners often go into alpha, but they don't stay there, though they still stay "high." And non-stoners go into alpha, and they don't consider themselves "high" at all, but rather quite clear, present and grounded. Most of us intuit that human consciousness is more complex, and more beautiful and more mysterious than merely what electro-chemical-magnetic brain-wave frequency we're momentarily tuned to, and/or broadcasting from. For example, what's the brain wave frequency for "maternal love"? Is it the same frequency for every mother, or the same frequency as love of country, or love of one's Chevy?

Ann Wise suggests that the "awakened mind" is one in which all frequencies are harmonized, "coherent," working as a single radiance. The Zen Master Huang Po, when asked what enlightenment was, replied, "your ordinary mind." Being high, being awake, being enlightened, falling in love, *being* love is more than just a matter of changing the brain's electro-chemical-magnetic frequency setting. Still, looking at brain waves gives us some basic, empirically documented data with which to start when we're looking at what it means to be stoned.

Stoned Rats and First Evidence of a Contact High

Back in the late 60's several of my close buddies--commune comrades--were graduate students working in micro-biology labs at our local university. One of their faculty mentors was Jay Best, Ph.D., an old-time tenured professor with an international reputation for cutting edge research. Because of his deep integrity, he had one of the few grants in the country from the National Institute of Health that allowed him to grow and study the effects of marijuana. Many of us were disappointed that he had been funded to study the effects of marijuana not on humans, but on *rats*. (Yes, of course: We laughed a lot and plotted about how we, too, might be able to "test" some of the righteous weed that was being grown for Dr. Best's study. Alas, we never succeeded. As might be expected, with the priorities the way they were, and are, the security and documentation around the inflow and outflow of every leaf of cannabis in that university green house was tighter than the security policies at Fort Knox or the local nuclear power plants. Besides, at the time, scoring righteous weed, at relatively inexpensive prices, was not difficult.)

One of the projects in which my buddies were involved was to help Dr. Best try to figure out how best to get the rats stoned. Cannabis, after all (and thank God) is not "injectable." At home, we made jokes about rolling up teeny tiny little "mouse joints." In the lab, they discovered that the "red oil" extracted from the cannabis plants (which included carbon-14 delta-9-tetrahydrocannabinol—*i.e.*, the "good stuff") when injected into the veins of the rats' tails, would clog up, not circulate up to the rat brain in which they had planted little wires—"indwelling intracranial electrodes"--to measure various rat brain waves. (Some of us English majors were a bit squeamish about the implanting of "indwelling intracranial electrodes" into their little rat brains, but that's another story.)

Dr. Best came up with an ingenious solution. He had one of the grad students feed large balls of pork fat, suet and hamburger to a few German Shepherd dogs (the German Shepherds loved it) and then, 10 to 30 minutes later, extract the resulting "fatty serum" from a vein in the dogs' front leg. This serum, mixed with controlled doses of the magical red oil, they then injected into the rat tails. Somehow it worked. The rats, according to their brain monitors, got stoned. (Dr. Best was a genius at intuiting such procedures.)

What they discovered (in simplified plain English, rather than in lab speak) was that under the influence of cannabis, **the rats' brainwave activity changed from the primarily dominant beta waves, to primarily dominant alpha waves**. And a bit more technically, they discovered ("tentatively") that the "order of firing" in the brain wave activity switched from originating in the hippocampus--when not stoned--to the septal nucleus, when stoned, *i.e.*, brainwave activity occurs in a slightly different sequence, from proximate but different parts of the brain when under the influence, at least for rats.

(On a side note, I once viewed a video--probably a super 8 movie--of Dr. Best's "stoned rat research." I had heard much about this movie but when I actually saw it was a bit disappointed. No mellow music, jive talking, no laughing or Woodstock-like grins or peace signs. Just slow moving rats. More specifically, two stoned rats, and two not stoned rats that had been placed on a stool. As one of my old buddies recalls it: "The two stoned rats wandered over to the edge of the stool they were on, lay down and gazed dreamily at the floor. And then, unexpectedly, the two control rats--the un-stoned rats--likewise wandered over to the edge of the stool and likewise lay down and gazed dreamily at the floor. Thus, the first documented evidence for the reality of a *contact high*!"—later explained by the discovery of "mirror neurons.")

Before the experiments could be concluded, let alone duplicated, Richard Nixon was elected President, and shortly thereafter all funding for marijuana research was abruptly ended. None of the observations or results from Dr. Best's work in this area were ever published. Nevertheless, later investigators found similar results.

"The most consistent effect of chronic marijuana consumption on EEG involves alterations in alpha waves in the frontal cortex," writes Mitch Earleywine in *Understanding Marijuana—a New Look at the Scientific Evidence*. (p.152) published by Oxford University Press in 2005. "Alpha waves...indicate a state of quiet relaxation. People with an average of 10 years of daily marijuana use show more power in these alpha waves. Their frontal alpha waves also show greater coherence, meaning that the left and right sides of their brains seem to emit these waves at the same time." Hmmm . . .

Where Did That Train Come From?

It seems clear then that when we get high (be it by pot, or by settling into the hot tub or taking a hike to the top of the mountain), alpha often jumps ahead of beta-- beta's still there, but alpha is dominant. Other research suggests that when we're high, we're not so attached to our thoughts; we're more into our senses, our "feeling of being."

With the slower alpha waves becoming more dominant, it follows that the even slower theta waves, too, then become more available. (Remember, theta waves are those when, as you fall asleep, relaxing deeper and deeper, thinking of the people and events of the day, when an image of, say, a little pig dressed in a blue dress appears, you know you're experiencing theta!)

The experience of being high is when we experience our thought trains coming and going unbidden. And at times, we recognize that some of these "stoned thought-trains" are perhaps quite bizarre, or funny, and actually have nothing to do with our hum-drum personal lives. We can take it a step further and sometimes observe that what we assumed were our own, personal, private thought trains are in fact quite "impersonal." Thought trains are arriving and leaving that we've never seen before! (This freaks out some folks.)

Pot and Short-Term Memory

As mentioned, when stoned, thoughts often begin firing from different places in our brain. Thus, our short term memory is temporarily interrupted. Which is great, if we've had a crummy day at work a "short term" ago. More often, we remember the work, but from a different angle, a different perspective. Such biological change seems helpful, useful; indeed, such change may even enhance our chances for survival. (As Bob Dylan sang, "Those not busy being born are busy dying!")

In our ordinary walk-around "beta state," most of us are deeply conditioned by and identified with thought trains of both the past and future. We're thinking about what we've just done, and/or what we need to do next. We're often engaged in goal oriented tasks, be they large or small, primarily dedicated to fixing what has happened in the past or preparing for what might happen in the future. The relatively rapid "beta mind" is generally a time-locked and time-driven state of mind.

Although in this beta mind we may be very "practical," balancing the checkbook or planning a barbecue, our thoughts are almost always on the past or future. Welcome to modern times.

Again, after a hit or two of smoke (or when we practice either of the first two Potless Pot High Games!) the slower, calmer "alpha" state begins to dominate the beta state. We begin working, perceiving from a different part of the brain. We start to perceive the moment's sensory input. Especially in the beginning, this change of state is often very subtle.

Learning to Get High

In an essay appearing in the book *Altered States of Consciousness*, edited by Charles Tart, one writer observes, that "persons unfamiliar with the marijuana state frequently must 'learn' that they are perceiving experience in a different way. That is, someone makes them aware of changed perception by showing them objects, playing music, and calling their attention to the difference in sights and sounds. Then they become consciously aware of the perceptual changes. This initiation procedure has led sociologist H. S. Becker… to suggest that most of the effects of marijuana are *learned*, not spontaneous. He says (accurately, I am sure) that the user must learn to notice the effects, categorize them, and connect them to the total experience of using the drug. What is learned in most cases is not a new way of perceiving, but the *awareness* of a change in perception…" (emphasis added.)

In the fifth Potless Pot High game (Chapter 16) we dive deeply into the differences between our "perceptions" and the awareness of our perceptions. It's a subtle investigation, yet with profound and powerful "get high" results.

But let's not get ahead of ourselves. It's first useful to ask, what *are* these changes in perception that come about due to the effects of weed? Becker writes:

> "The usual, most noticeable effect is intensification of sensation and increased clarity of perception. Visually, colors are brighter, scenes have more depth, patterns are more evident and figure-ground relations both more distinct and more easily reversible. Other sense modalities do not have the variety of visual stimuli, but all seem to be intensified. Sounds become more distinct, with the user aware of sounds he otherwise might not have

> noticed. Music, recorded and live, is heard with increased fidelity and dimension, as though there were less distance between the source and the listener. Taste and smell are also enhanced under marijuana. The spice rack is a treasure of sensation, and food develops a rich variety of tastes."

From my own direct research and from research of others, I am quite confident that that these enhanced sensations from the effects of weed are primarily because we have dropped or stood back from the *time-oriented mind* and come into the moment's reality! In other words, our body *always* feels and sees and hears and tastes in this "enhanced" way, but our mind is generally too busy to notice! Our busy mind habitually overrides and/or ignores what the body is constantly sensing.

Be Here Now

Few of us deeply experience on a regular basis what is simply happening in the moment. We seldom have the patience or "brain wave" acuity to tune into what we are actually seeing, or to actually taste what we are eating, even feel what we are feeling. We're too busy, too "beta." **The herb slows us down—from beta to alpha to theta—allowing us to simply be present with what is always already here!** It is not surprising in the beginning that most of us had to "learn" that we were indeed high, to become *aware* of what our bodies are actually experiencing.

When we ask the question, *"Do I enjoy riding this thought train, or am I at peace riding this thought train,"* the question itself slows us down, steps us back from the monkey mind, away from immersion in the thought stream. When we are brave enough to *choose* what we are entertaining in consciousness, and more precisely, when we allow our own momentary sense of peace and joy to guide our choices, we step out of the time-locked mind and into something deeper, more profound and more immediate.

But I'm getting ahead of myself here; back to the stoner brain waves. Getting stoned isn't always about slowing down, getting mellow--though often it is. Sometimes it's an experience of being quite inspired, speeding up, seeing life secrets or patterns that had previously been overlooked. Sometimes pot generates quite rapid brain waves. Ahh . . .

And Now for Those Sweet, Sweet Gammas:

What marijuana, alcohol, speed, cocaine, the hallucinogens, even heroin have in common--the basic attraction of the whole drug experience--at least on *some* occasions, is the possibility of taking us into the blissful gamma range. The drug experience, at its best, gives us--or more precisely releases in us--a "peak experience" in which we see ourselves and the world, past, present and future, as a single shimmering radiance: holy, profound, complete. We're in love. We *are* love. *This* is gamma.

And then a horn honks outside or the boss calls or we remember we were supposed to pick up the kids at the babysitters. We come down for one reason or another. The experience collapses. Indeed, the "peak experience" itself--the experience of wholeness, radiance, love--is not guaranteed every time a drug is ingested. In fact, after a while, it becomes somewhat rare. But it's what we're shooting for (so to speak.)

"The addiction is never to the substance itself," wrote David Hawkins, M.D., Ph.D. "but rather to the *state of consciousness* which the substance elicits . . ." (Hawkins, *Consciousness and Addiction* Tapes, Veritas Publishing)

Of all the drugs, pot seems to offer, if not a consistent "peak experience," then at least consistent access to a more mellow states of consciousness. Not necessarily the most intense, expansive, electric or profound--not always gamma--though at times and places it does indeed offer gateway into these higher visionary states. That's why so many people love to smoke it once in a while, or once a month, or once a week, or every day.

"The danger with heroin," an ex-con friend once remarked, "is that it's so nice, you just *have* to go back." Likewise, the danger of pot, once one learns to recognize its effects, is that it makes you giggle, laugh, love your buddy, or your sister, or view the sunset in a completely different way. And occasionally it gives us insight (seemingly) into the inner workings of the cosmos. Why is this dangerous? Because it makes us want to feel that way again. And again. And again.

As any long term pot smoker will attest, the access to gamma is not always guaranteed, and indeed, it seems that the more often we smoke, the less likely it is that the pot itself will lead us into such states. We--or more precisely our brains--are too "wonderfully made" to be so easily manipulated at will. Our inner workings are too mysterious, too profound, too transcendental to be truly or fully "completed" simply by ingesting this or that substance.

However, if we are engaged in other "clarifying" activities--improving our diet, (physical, emotional and mental,) training our mind, keeping good company, we are more likely to experience these higher visionary states more often, with or without pot. Indeed, the saints, monks, yogis and other holy seers appear to access these higher states, if not at will, then quite regularly. And very few of them are pot heads!

As mentioned at the start of this long chapter, getting high is *not* just about which brain wave is currently dominant, though brain wave frequencies can hint at what 's happening in there. Let's go a little deeper and look at what's happening to the cells and neurons in the brain when we get stoned. For that, though, we do need another chapter.

Chapter 7

Opening Our Brain Gates:

How Pot – and the Potless Games—
Dissolve Our Cultural Addictions

"The ego is nothing other than the focus of conscious attention."
--- Alan Watts

"A fully flexible central nervous system is not biased toward the high-arousal narrow-objective focus or the low arousal diffuse-immersed state. Instead, left to its own devices, the nervous system naturally cycles through these styles, along a spectrum, and combines the variety of attention styles." --- Les Fehmi, PhD, The Open Focus Brain

In the last chapter we looked at how pot changes the brainwaves—allowing (in general) the alpha state to come forward and the beta state to move to the background, with an occasional cameo appearance from those sweet, sweet gamma waves. Another way of describing this is that we move out of the narrow, primarily time-bound, project-oriented frame of mind, where everything is a means to an end, into a wider focus where we become aware that the means and the ends are the same! When stoned we are more inclined to recognize that life--with all of its delicious tastes and sounds and colors and textures--is happening *right here, right now*. We're already at our destination, and always have been. What a wonderful surprise!

Sensory Gating

To understand how this actually happens it will be useful now to look at another brain mechanism called "sensory gating." Here's a layman's, simplified description: When the brain first registers some stimulus, generally through the senses, its teeny little gates (synapses) are "open." In the milliseconds that it takes the brain to process new stimuli, it temporarily closes, or at least narrows its gates, so that it is not overwhelmed by the next stimulus. In our walk-around world we do the same thing when we turn down the radio in order to better focus on what our mate is saying.

Here's Professor Mitch Earlywine's more scientific description of the gating process: "The p50 is a positive brain wave that appears about 50 milliseconds after people hear a clicking sound. When two clicks are presented quickly, one right after the other...[the] brain generates a normal P50 wave after the first click, but because the person is still processing the first click, the P50 in the second click is smaller than usual. It's as if the brain filters out some aspect of the second click while it processes the first one. The smaller response to the second click is sometimes referred to as gating, as if the brain closes a gate while processing the first click so that new information from the second click does not interfere...."

Referencing a particular study of heavy pot users, Earlywine goes on: "Chronic users of cannabis have reduced gating.... In the study, users had smoked an average of 13 joints per week for an average of 13.5 years....The users showed significantly less P50 gating than nonusers." (*Understanding Marijuana—a New Look at the Scientific Evidence*, p. 153)

In other words, it seems as if pot keeps the gates open! And yes, maybe for long term heavy users the gates might get stuck open! Nevertheless, this "open gate" state of mind, (or state of brain!) helps explain why colors seem more vivid, sounds more detailed, tastes and sights more alive! And why our ideas seem more vibrant, more powerful! More stuff is coming through the gate!

And this process also helps explain why after a while we want to shut down, close the gates, take a nap—or just sit on the couch, watch TV. Our brains have been working overtime—too much traffic coming through the gates. We need to retreat.

Again, back to the layman's descriptions: When we get stoned, the world seems to open up. We experience a change in the nature of our attention. (Isn't that why we do it?)

Following Alan Watts' insight, it makes sense that such a change of attention, such an opening, is also going to change our ego structure. (Again, what a relief, at least temporarily!) This change in the ego structure is why some rare people, perhaps already inclined toward ego fragmentation, have experienced deeply troubling psychological breakdowns--meltdowns--after imbibing the herb.

Of course, rather than an unhealthy inner melt down, many others have experienced what feels like a healthy inner "coming together" via the herb. But for a moment, let's look a little closer at the meltdowns. (We have to admit, my stoner friends, such meltdowns do happen. Rather than deny, let's get curious as to *why*.)

Uncomfortable Mental Meltdowns

Such meltdowns seem to occur because there's too much traffic coming through the brain gates. In *Marijuana and Madness*, edited by David Castle and Robin Murray, we find very technical, quite clinical (read, "somewhat boring") descriptions and analyses of this meltdown process. Castle and Murray have collected high-level research documenting how those diagnosed with active or latent neurotic, psychotic and/or schizophrenic behaviors will often see such behaviors magnified when under the influence of weed. (Not fair to summarize the whole deeply nuanced and clinically useful book in a single sentence, or paragraph, but there it is.)

The gates get opened. We generally don't even hear or at least generally don't pay attention to, don't believe the strange voices in our head, but with the "open gates" of pot, such voices can take on a new vibrancy, even urgency. Thus the rare incidences of psychosis, or psychotic breaks after imbibing the weed. Curiously, some folks diagnosed with schizophrenia or schizoid-affective disorders migrate to pot as a way of self-medicating. Even though it widens the gates, pot seems to soften the voices, make them more gentle, more friendly. Perhaps it's the difference between "beta" voices and "alpha" voices.

Let's remind ourselves that it's not just pot that can cause such "breaks" or meltdowns. Such events have also been known to be triggered by too much Pepsi, or a screaming mother-in-law or the lack of sunshine, or a cross word from a fast-food server. The study of human behavior, and particularly our mental processes, is still an inexact science.

As a side note, my own experience in sharing the Potless Games with various friends and clients who have been diagnosed with such mental maladies, is that by following our own native joy, following our own peace (by asking *"do I enjoy riding this thought train, am I at peace with this thought train, yes or no"*), the gates open and close in a timely, harmonious manner. Our own sense of joy and peace become the "regulators" or guardians for the inner gates of consciousness (the doors of perception, as Aldous Huxley put it.)

More specifically, when we practice the first two games, consciously, intentionally magnifying our ordinary joy and peace, we find ourselves naturally more open, more receptive, more in tune with our surroundings, much more so than if we are angry, uptight or depressed. One of my friends, diagnosed with severe bi-polar disorder and at one time, to use his words, "a resident of every nut house in a six state area," also a grower and user of medicinal marijuana, reported, "I haven't had one of those deep [manic or depressive] spikes in over 16 months," after taking up the first two Potless Games. For him, it was the longest "normal" time he had experienced in many decades.

But again I get ahead of myself. Back to the brain, and open and closed gates, or what might more practically be understood as open and closed *styles of attention.*

The Open-Focus Brain

Les Fehmi and Jim Robbins, in their ground-breaking book, *The Open Focus Brain,* document how our culture—western culture in general—inculcates a "narrow focus" style of attention as our daily walk-around style of attention. From our earliest years we are encouraged and trained to adopt a "narrow focus," whether that focus is on school work, sporting moves, household chores or career objectives. Fehmi is quick to point out that such a narrow focus can be quite useful, even necessary on occasion for our very survival.

"Evolution," Fehmi writes, "provided humans with this narrow beam of attention to respond, in the short run, to urgent or important external situations. There's nothing inherently wrong with it; in fact, one reason it is overused is precisely because it is so helpful and allows us, in the short run, to accomplish so much. What's wrong is our near-complete dependence on it and addiction to it."

Our near-complete cultural *addiction* to narrow focus? Hmmm… Might pot in fact be helping us *break* such a cultural addiction? Thus the "counter-culture?"

Fehmi points out that "narrow-focus" attention is generally an 'emergency' mode of attention that "substantially increases the frequency of the brain's electrical activity." Having been trained in "narrow focus," we habitually function in survival mode—urgency mode—from morning to night. Thus our high stress levels, and thus our many ailments, from obesity to heart disease to divorce and prescription drug dependence.

In their book *Nudge --- Improving Decisions About Health, Wealth and Happiness---* psychologists Richard Thaler, from the University of Chicago, and Cass Sunstein, from Harvard, suggest there are two types, or systems of thinking, or attention: the Automatic System, and the Reflexive System. They offer this tidy chart:

The Automatic System	**The Reflective System**
uncontrolled	controlled,
effortless	effortful
associative	deductive
fast	slow
unconscious	self-aware
skilled	rule following

Their two systems might otherwise be neatly labeled open, or "stoned" (the "automatic system") and closed, or "not stoned (the "reflexive system.") Although most of us have a natural, or cultural, or familial inclination toward one or the other "system" of thinking, or style of attention, we are all capable of thinking—mentally processing--- using either of the systems.

We can also observe that we each have thousands of subtle variations of "styles" of mental processing between these two systems. The line is not as clear and clean cut as the table would make it. And the differences in style of attention, or in ways of thinking, between when we are stoned or not stoned cannot be so precisely (narrowly!) defined as the difference between "open" and "closed."

Nevertheless, looking at the brain waves, the neurological gates, and the psychological research into "systems of thinking," the terms "open and closed" appear fairly accurate. This helps explain why, amongst stoners, there is a shared perception of a "closed minded society"--the non-stoner society--that is suppressing, oppressing the open experimentation (and open lifestyle) that they, we, are engaging.

Let's return for a moment to the opening quotation for this chapter, and the idea expressed by Les Fehmi: *A fully flexible central nervous system is not biased toward the high-arousal narrow-objective focus or the low arousal diffuse-immersed state. Instead, left to its own devices, the nervous system naturally cycles through these styles, along a spectrum, and combines the variety of attention styles.*

Let's juxtapose this idea with Andrew Weil's observation:

> "We seem to be born with a drive to experience episodes of altered consciousness. This drive expresses itself at very early ages in all children in activities designed to cause loss or major disturbance of ordinary awareness.... To an outside, adult observer these practices seem very perverse and even dangerous, but in most cases adults have simply forgotten their own identical experiences as children.... Thus, use of illegal drugs is nothing more than a logical continuation of a developmental sequence going back to early childhood. It cannot be isolated as a unique phenomenon of adolescence, of contemporary America, of cities, or of any particular social or economic class."[1]

Fehmi calls the movement between "open and closed" styles of attention a "natural cycling." Weil names it, a "logical continuation of a developmental sequence." Moving from closed to open, from beta to alpha, from not stoned to stoned, is not just "escapism." It may indeed be a biological urge, *i.e.*, a healthy impulse! Rather than try to suppress this urge, let's honor it.

Back to the Potless Pot High Games: We can observe that for many long-time potheads the problem seems to be that the "developmental sequence" has become stalled, or at

---

[1] from "*The Natural Mind: A New Way of Looking at Drugs and the Higher Consciousness,*" by Andrew Weil, Houghton Mifflin Company, Boston, (1972) ISBN: 0-395-13936-8

least slowed to a frustrating pace. Where pot once took them—us--into new territories, to exciting insights and what felt like unfolding awareness, they/we now often experience getting high as a mostly pleasant routine that leads to the *"same ol' same ol' "* levels of consciousness. In the same way, an old joke may still be funny, but it *is* an old joke! Let's move on! We already know the punch line.

For those who once came to pot then went away, the "developmental sequence"--the urge toward a change in consciousness--may have taken the form of vocational urgency, or ambition, or family engagements or sports or hobbies or church or synagogue. So be it. Here, too, as with the pot high, it's possible for the "continuation of our developmental sequences"--the urge toward a change in consciousness--to become stuck, stalled, or at least slowed to a frustrating pace. Our very biology calls out for more "brain wave changes."

In these last few chapters we have taken a brief (very brief!) glimpse at a hundred years of research, and fifty years of intense sociological experience that documents that when people get stoned on pot, they consistently, almost inevitably get easy, mellow, inspired. The edges comes off. They grin, get goofy and relaxed. Again, *almost* inevitably. These are the consistent effects (in layman's terms) of cannabis. That's why it's the drug of choice for such a large (mostly underground) population.

But as any stoner knows, it's not always cool, or fun, to smoke a bowl before going in for our annual review at work, or when we need to clean out the septic tank (very similar tasks.) Cleaning the septic tank, we don't necessarily want our gates "wide open" in such an arena. But we want to be happy with our boss, and we want to be efficient, stay peaceful, when cleaning the septic tank. So how do we do this, without smoking a bowl?

Read on--

Chapter 8

Stoned While Doing the Laundry:

Beyond Positive Thinking: Tips for Daily Practice

" A mind all logic is like a knife all blade. It makes the hand bleed that uses it."

---- Rabindranath Tagore

In the next chapter we'll continue to look at the physiological effects of pot, and why it is in fact "medicinal" for so many people, whether they have a doctor's prescription or not. But after those last two somewhat "brainy" chapters, it seems wise to get back to basics, back to the games. We need a break. Let's get high again!

How? In my experience, we can't remind ourselves too often that enjoying our happiness really *is* the most important thing we can do for ourselves and all those around us, the most loving thing we can do. Experiencing our joy is even more important than understanding the neuro-physiological effects of cannabis, as useful as that understanding may be.

And being at peace really *is* the most practical thing we can do in *every* circumstance and *every* relationship. Isn't this why we decide to get stoned, or decide to *not* get stoned? Either way, we're wanting to enjoy our happiness more, wanting to experience our peace more. For some folks, smoking a bowl is *not* a happy event, is not a peaceful procedure. For others it seems to be.

We can easily observe that we enjoy ourselves--stoned or not stoned--only when we are enjoying the train of thought we are riding. We are at peace only when we are at peace with the train of thoughts and stories we are telling ourselves and others. There's no other way.

Other Things More Important?

When spelled out in simple words, most people quickly agree that enjoying our happiness, and being at peace is obviously the most important thing we can do for ourselves and those around us. Nevertheless, we often forget such basic insights during our daily round of affairs, allowing a myriad of other things to become more important, assuming other things to be more practical than our own joy and peace. We get lost in our work deadlines, in the commute, in the grocery shopping, finding a babysitter. Welcome to modern times.

So in the "get high" games we're playing in order to stay in our joy, stay in our peace, we simply ask, whenever necessary, *do I enjoy riding this thought train, yes or no,* or *am I at peace with telling this story, yes or no*. If the answer is not an immediate and spontaneous *yes,* then it's a *no*.

In these games, if the answer is *yes,* that's perfect. We are at peace. We're enjoying ourselves. If the answer is no (*I do not enjoy riding this thought train, I am not at peace with these thought trains,*) then in order to return to peace, return to joy, we choose one of two options:

a. drop or jump off the thought trains or stories with which we are not at peace, or which we are not enjoying, and then find or create thought trains and stories which we enjoy more, or with which we are more at peace;

or

b. choose to enjoy the thought train, or be at peace with the story that a moment before we did not enjoy, with which we were not at peace.

Guaranteed: If you play these inner games, employ this inner cognitive process, you *will* get high, if only a little, and then a little more! Your brains waves *will* change. Your alpha will become more dominant. Your inner gates will open. Your daily life will take on more glow!

Again, in my experience the *idea* that enjoying our happiness is important and the *idea* that being at peace is practical--these simple ideas often start out as a somewhat impersonal "philosophy" or maybe just nice theories. However, as we test the ideas, test the philosophy, test the theories in our own daily walk-around experience, **what begins as an idea, or a theory, gradually becomes a *real-time personal observation*..** as real as the observation that it is raining.

My gosh, yes, peace of mind really is very practical! Enjoying my happiness really is the most important, most loving thing I can do for myself and others. **When these ideas move from an impersonal theory to a direct personal *observation*, the games become empowered.** The space ship has launched!

So let's see if we can bring these ideas out of the "theory" realm into our daily round of affairs. We can start by simply observing that it's usually a lot easier to enjoy ourselves when we're out to dinner with friends, or at a movie or a party, or maybe skiing down the slopes or lying on a tropical beach. Our brain waves have been changed. We're much more open. It's obviously easier to enjoy ourselves or be at peace in these situations, though of course such joy and peace are not guaranteed by such outer circumstances.

Most of our lives, however, are filled with much more mundane activities, like setting the kitchen table, mowing the lawn, meeting work deadlines, driving to the store. What should we do about these more mundane chores, which are in fact our more common experience?

As mentioned in earlier chapters, I first learned the Freedom Game from Christian Almayrac, the French physician who was on a 20 state lecture tour. He was being billed as "Dr. Happiness." One day I asked Dr. Almayrac about these chores, these "mundane" times. I remember the example I gave.

"What about those neutral times," I asked. "Like when we're ironing?"

Dr. Almayrac smiled and responded, (duh): *"If it's not an immediate and spontaneous yes, it's a no."*

If we don't enjoy ironing, let's not iron! Or let's change how we're thinking about it. If we don't enjoy the commute, are not at peace with the project deadline, we are free *not* to do these things. And we are likewise free to change how we're thinking about them. (That's why it's called the *freedom* game.)

When we recognize in our daily lives that experiencing joy and peace truly *is* the most important, most fundamental, most loving thing we can do for ourselves and those around us, then we will find the courage we need to align all our thoughts and acts with what we know to be true.

Yes, of course, it's important to find a babysitter, it's important to show up for work on time, it's practical to pay the utility bill. These are all important and practical aspects of our ordinary daily lives. Yet they are not the *most* important thing we can do, not the *most* practical thing we can do. It's most important to *enjoy* showing up for work on time, it's most practical to be at *peace* with the grocery shopping! These are the types of relationships and circumstances that make up *most* of our ordinary daily lives. **If we aren't enjoying these daily mundane events, if we aren't at peace with these ordinary relationships, we're cheating ourselves out of life's deep (mundane!) deliciousness!**

I've known stoners who get stoned to do the laundry, or do the grocery shopping, or to mow the lawn. Yes, it often happens after smoking a bowl that they then get sidetracked or forget the grocery list or leave big swaths of grass down the middle. Other times, though, such chores are done with more precision, patience and artistry than if they hadn't been stoned. The point here is that they get stoned before doing such chores because they want to enjoy themselves more throughout their *whole* lives. They don't want to be at war with their chores.

We too can "get high" while doing our daily chores, engaging our daily round of affairs, when we simply cease thinking about them in ways that we don't enjoy. When we *intentionally* drop the thought trains and stories with which we are not at peace and find the stories with which we are more at peace, or choose to enjoy what a moment before we didn't enjoy, we are intentionally changing our brain waves.

We can train ourselves to enjoy doing the dishes, or to be at peace with the month end report, or attending the PTA board meeting, though it is not common in our culture to do this. What is common is to postpone our joy, postpone our peace until after the PTA meeting, after the month-end report is done. But life's too short to postpone enjoying it. PTA meetings and month-end reports may be important, but they are *not* more important than peace on earth, or bringing joy to the world.

Are We Being *Pollyannaish*?

Yes, yes, of course, this sounds very Pollyannaish. As might be assumed, Dr. Almayrac was often accused of this very thing. Being from France, he wasn't familiar with the book Pollyanna---the classic children's book by Eleanor Porter which came out in the early part of the 1900's and from which a classic movie was made.

For those who are not familiar, the book is about a young girl, Pollyanna who plays what she calls "the glad game" wherever she goes, whoever she's with. It's a game she learned from her father, a Christian missionary, who told her that there were over 800 verses in the Bible in which God tells us to rejoice or be glad. Having been accused of being "Pollyannaish" time and time again, Dr. Almayrac found a copy of the book and read it. His response?

"Yes, Pollyanna had it exactly right!" he said excitedly. "She was a very brave girl. And very intelligent. I loved this book!" He was happy—or at least at peace—when he was associated with Pollyanna.

And yet, in our current day the term *Pollyannaish* has evolved to imply someone who is naïve, foolish, unrealistic, someone who doesn't have their feet planted firmly on the ground. (Let's remember that "reality" for lemmings is occasionally what makes them run en masse over the cliff into the sea. "Reality" is what led the Germans to believe they were the master race, and the Russians to suffer for over 50 years under communism. Being bravely unrealistic relative to the rest of our culture can sometimes be the wisest, most loving course.)

Beyond Positive Thinking

Let's be clear here: neither the Freedom Game nor the Peace Practice are mere restatements of the old "positive thinking" game--- or Pollyanna's "glad game", though at first glance that's how they may appear. And as those who are experienced can testify, the "get high" experience itself is not simply an experience of uninterrupted positive thinking.

Here's the difference: **Thought trains, of themselves, are neither positive nor negative,** neither happy nor unhappy, neither peaceful nor un-peaceful. Joy and peace are qualities that are *prior* to thinking. We are inherently capable of bringing joy and peace to our thought trains--*any* thought train. Or we can get lost in our thoughts.

We dive deeper into this when we look at awareness itself in Chapter 16, but for now let's look at some basic examples. I may enjoy the thought train: "*I think I'll drink a six pack, get naked and drive my motorcycle a hundred miles an hour across the prairie.*" I may enjoy such a thought train. I can assure you that my dear 99 year old Aunt Harriet would not enjoy such a thought train. Same train of thought. Different feelings about it.

And then let's say I enjoy that thought train so much that I actually act on it —drink a six'er, ride my rocket naked across the prairies. And then of course, it starts to rain, and the state patrol sees me, and I'm pulled over and soon I'm sitting in the slammer wrapped in a blanket. Now the thought train about drinking and riding and being naked is probably not so attractive.

The point here is that **the thought trains we enjoy on one day we might not enjoy the next day**. Or what we enjoy in one moment we might not enjoy the next moment. And visa versa, the thought trains we don't enjoy today we might enjoy tomorrow. Here's the key: Although it appears that these games are focused on what we are thinking, the true focus is on what we are feeling, and more particularly, about the presence or absence of the feeling of joy and peace.

Because it's so important, let me repeat a subtle, but very powerful insight that comes from playing the Potless Pot High Games: **thought trains themselves are neither happy nor unhappy, peaceful nor un-peaceful.** We are either happy to ride those trains or not. We are at peace with them or not. And this can change in a moment!

The most obvious example of this can be found in sports. "The Dallas Cowboys are a better team than the Washington Redskins." True or not true, this is a thought train that people from Dallas might enjoy, while the folks in Washington might not. Same thought train. We just bring different "identities" to it. Curiously, we can do the same with *any* thought train: if we aren't enjoying it, if we aren't at peace with it, we can bring a different identity to it!

This is true with thought trains about the laundry, about grocery shopping, the monthly report, and the utility bill. Again, when we recognize that enjoying our happiness, being at peace, really *is* the most important thing we can do for ourselves and those around us, we release our hold on various accumulated "mundane" identities in order to experience our deeper, more natural identity—the one that is naturally happy, at peace.

So let's back up and talk for a moment about "positive and negative" thinking. For a hundred years we have been encouraged to "drop" our negative thinking and adopt positive thinking. The hidden power in this comes from the fact that we most often *enjoy* positive thought trains more than negative thought trains; we are often more at peace with positive thinking than we are with negative thinking. But not always. And again, it's not black and white. What may be "positive' for one person may seem "negative" to another.

We've all known people who are so "positive" that we wanted to pinch them. Their positive demeanor can seem somehow unnatural, unreal, "put on."

Life is complex. Sometimes negative thought trains are much more appropriate than positive ones. For example, research suggests that most children, by the age of four, have heard the word "*no*" over 600,000 times, and rightfully so. That *is* a hot stove, that *is* Aunt Martha's delicate vase.

If/when we tell our child "*no, don't touch Aunt Martha's vase, it might brea*k" and we are *enjoying* ourselves, if we are at peace with ourselves, then the child will more easily listen and obey. On the other hand, if we tell the child "*no, don't touch Aunt Martha's vase, it might break*" and we are *not* enjoying ourselves, not at peace, even though we use the exact same words, the child does not enjoy such a command, is not at peace with such a demand because she is picking up our own feelings! She is then much more likely to challenge us.

The same thing happens with our grown-up family, friends and colleagues. There are times when it's perfectly appropriate to think—and speak—negative thoughts. For example, we might tell our boss, " No, I'm not going to work over-time again tonight, you slave driver. I've got a date. Besides, I've already worked late six times in the last ten days!" If when we utter such a negative sentiment we do so from a place of natural joy or peace, our boss will more easily accept it than if we utter *the exact same words* but are unhappy, at war.

Or let's say we tell our college age son, "You slacker. I've seen enough of your laundry. I'm old. It's time you take over that chore." If we are able to offer such words with a grin on our face, and *genuine* joy, we're going to get a grin in return. On the other hand, if we say the exact same words and are angry and uptight, we're going to get "angry and uptight" in return.

Here's the point: **We can sometimes enjoy negative thinking,** negative thought trains, Our joy, our peace is *not* confined only to "positive thinking." We can stay with our joy and peace through the highs and lows and in-betweens of the thinking spectrum!

This is also the secret to why positive thinking "works" sometimes and sometimes it doesn't. If we are *enjoying* our affirmations, our positive statements, or at least are at peace with them, then we give them life. But if we are doubting and fearful and uncertain about our positive affirmations, they won't work!

We have seen this work out especially in cases where people are working with "positive affirmations" in cases where their physical health is at risk. If we repeat "*I am healthy I am healthy I am healthy*" while secretly feeling, "*I'm scared I'm scared I'm scared,*" whichever statement has the most *feeling* to it will win out.

Again, thought trains themselves (such as *I am going to do the laundry*) are neither happy nor unhappy, peaceful nor un-peaceful. It's what we *bring* to the thought train that counts—and we can choose what we'll bring, or at least what we'll cling to. When we cling to life's joy, life's peace, the rest of life's junk will gracefully take care of itself, guaranteed. When we stay with our joy, our peace, we are being brave, and doing what's best for ourselves and all those around us.

Sure, the question naturally arises, does such a strategy hold true even with the appearance of serious illness, or calamity or the prospect of death itself. Yes, it does, but to look deeper at these questions we'll need another chapter.

Chapter 9

Why (Almost) All Pot Use Is Medicinal:

Pot, the Potless Games, and the New Healing Modalities

"A merry heart doeth good like a medicine: but a broken spirit drieth the bones." Proverbs 17:22

We have an 82 year old neighbor, George, who has suffered from lower back pain most of his adult life. Naturally, over the years he tried all manner of medications, all manner of therapies, trying to alleviate the constant ache. Several months ago his doctor wrote him a prescription (actually, an "advisory") for medicinal marijuana, which is legal here in Colorado.

"For the first time in 50 years I found relief," he said. "It's a miracle. I thank God. I never again want to be without it."

Obviously, weed does not act like a miracle drug for everybody with lower back pain, nor for the other various ailments for which it has been prescribed ("advised"). And George himself will undoubtedly find that it works better some days than others. But George's experience--his relief from chronic pain--is not unique. Both the clinical and anecdotal evidence for the ameliorative effects of marijuana for a wide rainbow of physical maladies is inarguable.

We're preaching to the choir here. If you're this far into this book, and have an interest in going beyond pot into weedless enlightenment, you are undoubtedly educated enough about the herb to know the (valid) arguments for and (political) arguments against its medical uses. Very solid research has proven its beneficial effects for use

- As an anti-nauseant for those undergoing chemotherapy
- for loss of appetite due to AIDS and other wasting diseases
- as an anti-convulsant for spinal injuries,
- for relief of some of the symptoms of multiple sclerosis and epilepsy
- as an analgesic for chronic pain from cancer,
- for relief from migraine
- for relief for rheumatism
- for relief from symptoms of a variety of auto-immune diseases.

To withhold, because of cultural prejudice and ignorance or denial of accumulated scientific research, the relief that pot can offer from those suffering these ailments is, to my mind, criminal.

Organizations Supporting Medicinal Use

Although the American Medical Association, guardian of "narrow focus" medical authority, has not yet had the courage to speak up for the medicinal use of marijuana, the AMA's counterpart across the ocean, the British Medical Association has strongly supported such use, as have many state and local medical associations, such as the New York and New Mexico Medical Societies and the California and Florida Medical Associations. Even the very conservative Texas Medical Association has found enough evidence to publicly support medicinal use of marijuana. Other supporters of medicinal marijuana include such prestigious "science based" and politically neutral organizations as The American Public Health Association, The National Association of Public Health Policy, The

American Nurses Association, The American Academy of HIV Medicine, The Lymphoma Foundation of America and the National Nurses Society on Addictions. The list goes on and on. Again, evidence for the medicinal use of marijuana, for any objective observer, is inarguable.

For most readers of this book the question is *not* whether this wonderful herb actually does help those suffering with these and other ailments. Here's the problem:

"Good news, Doc, I've found that pot actually helps relieve my arthritis pain."

"Sorry Wilbur, my medical training does not allow me to believe you. As medical authorities we have not yet authorized a sufficient number of double blind studies that can be replicated in laboratory settings that would eventually offer sufficient evidence for your claim."

"But doc, it's doesn't hurt anymore."

"Sorry. Your direct experience doesn't count. Here, try these drugs from Big Pharma. "

But people's direct experiences--our friends' direct experiences—*do* count. We can choose to believe them. Of course pot helps, if not for everyone then for many. The interesting question here for those of us this far down the road isn't *if* pot helps in a wide variety of circumstances. Rather, *how* does it help? *Why*? Is it because marijuana ingestion triggers a purely physiological electro-chemical reaction that relieves a wide variety of biological ailments, or is there something deeper, maybe something simpler that is happening here, that is helping with the healing, from which we can learn?

First, let's be clear that that pot *does* have its basic physiological and biological healing (and occasionally damaging) components. But, as with all things physiological and biological, it's not black and white and it can be quite complex. The physiological effects can differ widely according to different individual body chemistries or even different circumstances. Bodies are complex and the effects of pot itself are complex. For example, as most every pot smoker knows, after first toking up the heart rate increases by 20 to 50 beats per minute, which can increase blood pressure. An increased heart rate--that first rush--can be hazardous. Some researchers suggest our chance of heart attack is many times greater during that first "lift off" because of the increased heart rate. But then again, we are encouraged by sports trainers to regularly exercise to a point where we can feel our heart rate beating faster. Is speeding up the heart good or bad for us? It depends...

After the initial speeding up of the heart, curiously, blood pressure often drops. One advocate claims he was able over several months to drop his high blood pressure by twenty points using only marijuana. Others have found similar results. Alas, some find it increases blood pressure. Again, the bio-physiology is complex, and quite individual.

Same thing holds true with marijuana as a "bronchial dilator." Researchers use a "peak flow device" to measure the amount of air lungs are capable of exhaling, and take readings both before and after marijuana is smoked. Such measurements confirm that marijuana does act as a short term "bronchial dilator," though the effects of the smoke itself might abrogate this in the long term. Marijuana brownies--or other cooked foods—alleviate the smoke problem.

It's not our intent here to debate or make an argument for the medicinal use of marijuana, though the argument is there for the making. Our quest here is of a more subtle nature. Sure, we want to get healthy, stay healthy, but we also want to get high, clear and spunky *without* the use of pot. So we're looking here at the medical effects in order to better understand how pot functions so that we might magnify similar functions in our "potless" games.

Summarizing our earlier exploration in previous chapters of the effects of pot on the brain and nervous system, we might say that pot tends to open the psyche a bit, change our focus from narrow to wide. Pot takes us out of the time-locked "becoming" state into a more present "being" state of mind. Or even more simply, pot helps us feel good, laugh, relax, not take ourselves or the world so damned seriously. And this, come to find out, is good for our health.

Being and Becoming

First, let's look at "being" in relation to "becoming." We might notice that our bodies are always functioning only in the *now,* can only *be* in the now. Nevertheless, most of the time for most of us, our minds are habitually focused on the future or on the past. So most of us habitually neglect what our bodies are feeling and doing and needing *right now.* As we've discussed, pot tends to bring us back into the now, back into our sensations, our direct momentary experience.

Curiously, this in itself is a healthy, healing way of being. We are giving our bodies time and space to do what bodies want to do—just *be,* just move, just feel, dance, laugh, love, *right now,* not later. This mind-set of "allowance" is in itself quite healthy. When we agree to be with our bodies, to simply be here enjoying the moment, our bodies can relax, smile, regenerate.

Similarly, when we ask, *"Do I enjoy riding this thought train,"* or *"Am I at peace with these stories,"* we are coming back to now, paying more attention to this moment's sensations, this moment's experience. The questions require us to pause and to simply *be* here while we observe our own immediate inner experience. This pause, this return to now, is healthy. Welcome home.

There are traditions and teachers who urge us to be with *whatever* thought train happens to come up, *whatever* feelings are here. Such teachings are useful in so far as they, too, bring us back into the moment. And yet, as Proverbs reminds us, "As a man thinketh in his heart, so is he," or the even more helpful Proverb, quoted at the beginning of this chapter, "a merry heart doeth good like a medicine, but a broken spirit (e.g unhappy, un-peaceful) drieth the bones."

"I been rich and I been poor," said Sophie Tucker, "and believe me honey, rich is better." We have thought trains we enjoy to ride and thought trains we don't enjoy. The ones we enjoy feel better, and are healthier.

William James wrote, "The greatest discovery of my generation is that a human being can alter his life by altering his attitudes of mind." Carlos Castaneda put it, "The world is such and such or so and so only because we tell ourselves that that is the way it is." And relative to health, N.S. Chamfort put it this way: "If taking vitamins doesn't keep you healthy enough, try more laughter".

Health Through Grins

It's not just philosophers and psychologists who point us toward the health benefits of a joyous, peaceable mindset. An article by Peggy Rynk for CBS reported on a wide variety of academic studies that confirm that mood and attitude influence health. For example, researchers from the University of California at Los Angeles found that the immune systems of actors could be influenced by the emotions they portrayed. The immune system was strengthened when the actors played a cheerful, upbeat role. The immune system was depressed when actors played somber, tragic roles. So even if we're *pretending* to be happy or sad, our health can be affected.

And if we're *not* pretending or faking our mood the effects are even worse (or better!) A long term study of 1300 men in and around Boston found that those who were habitually angry were three times more likely to suffer heart disease than those who were not. And researchers at the University of Chicago followed a group of 200 senior executives who were laid off by major telecommunications firms. Less than a third of those who saw this as a new opportunity and reason to "move on" with their lives experienced serious illness after the lay-off. Yet over 90% those who were frightened and angry about being "downsized" experienced some kind of major health challenge. 90%! (Remember our example for the Freedom

Game, *"You're fired!"* How we respond, how we play the Game can be life and death important!)

And further--researchers at Duke University followed medical students who had been tested in the 1950's for their attitude toward life. The students were put into two broad groups labeled hostile or friendly. By the time of the follow-up study thirty years later in the 1980's, those who had been viewed as more "hostile" towards life were much more likely to have died than those who were friendly. **Our basic attitude can make the difference between life and death.**

As one might suspect, in my daily work as a tobacco cessation counselor many of my clients were sent to me by their doctors, so many showed up with very dire diagnoses, including cancer, heart disease and COPD . (Most of my clients, I'm happy to report did *not* have such dire diagnoses.) I always looked for an opportunity to remind those clients with dire diagnoses that **there is no ailment anywhere in the world--from brain cancer to kidney failure to Bubonic Plague--that somebody somewhere hasn't reversed. Even the most "incurable" of diagnoses have been cured at one time or another, by somebody**. Our medicine is still an inexact science and the powers of the human body and mind have yet to be fully tapped.

Back to how the research on health and happiness relates to our quest. If weed and/or the potless games do indeed make us more friendly toward ourselves and others, less angry, more open to opportunities, we will be much more likely to live longer, and live healthier. And for some people, the simple "change in mood," the uplifting of spirits which pot elicits can have an *immediate* effect--an immediate uplift, like it did for George--on their physical condition as well.

As we've seen in previous chapters, pot does change the brain waves, pot does move the locus of perception; it opens us up, mellows us out. This change bodes well for our health.

This is not to say that we don't have crabby pot heads amongst us. Or cynical or angry or self-deprecating pot heads amongst us. Although pot tends to move our alpha in front of our beta, our habitual cultural uptight attitudes can and do easily block pot's mellowing effects. Nevertheless, any police officer will quickly tell you that she would much rather deal with someone who has indulged in a night of heavy pot smoking than someone who has indulged in a night of heavy drinking--- the pot smoker will be much more mellow 99% of the time!

Health Related to Modes of Attention

Les Fehmi, the psychologist and researcher mentioned earlier as the author of *The Open Focus Brain*, has found that people who are trained to pay attention in a new "open" manner, or style, rather than the traditional narrow focus of attention, often find relief from long standing physical ailments, including migraine headaches, asthma, nerve damage, arthritis and a poor golf stroke! His work has demonstrated that a change in the way we pay attention can have a dramatic effect on the way our body functions.

Likewise, way back in the 1930's and 1940's, William Bates, M.D. found that the way we pay attention can have a significant effect on something as basic and seemingly "hard wired" as our eyesight. "The fact is, that when the mind is at rest, nothing can tire the eyes," he wrote. "And when the mind is under strain, nothing can rest them. Anything that rests the mind will benefit the eyes." And maybe benefit the heart, the liver and gall bladder.

Gene Gendlin, from the University of Chicago, has been teaching a process he calls "focusing," which might better be termed, "releasing," or simply "listening." Gendlin teaches his students how to adopt a more friendly approach to the aches and pains and stimulations of their minds and bodies, rather than interpreting such discomforts as a "call to battle." The body wants to heal itself, wants to move in harmony and ease. Much of the inner healing work is to simply get out of the way and let the body find its natural, healthy state. We often "get in the way" of our own healing with the stories we tell ourselves, and the stories we accept from others.

"The physical world, including our bodies, is a response of the observer," observes Deepak Chopra. The response of the observer is a response in thought. He goes on, "We create our bodies as we create the experience of our world." And even more simply, he says, "***To think is to practice brain chemistry***." (Emphasis added.)

I often tell my clients that if they had to pay for the chemicals which the brain releases whenever they laugh, they couldn't afford to laugh. These brain chemicals are powerful healing agents. The old saying really is true: laughter *is* the best medicine!

"Imagine a world in which medicine was oriented towards healing rather than disease," wrote Andrew Weil, MD. "Where doctors believed in the natural healing capacity of human beings and emphasized prevention over treatment. In such a world, doctors and patients would be partners working toward the same end."

Joy Heals

Dr. Christian Almayrac, previously mentioned as the "discoverer" of the Freedom Game, found that when his patients began practicing their joy as a beginning, daily *discipline,* rather than as a hoped-for end-result of some activity or circumstance, then the other modalities he was prescribing appeared to have more effect. Practicing their joy, many of his patients were able to reduce their reliance on other medications, and many experienced quicker, more lasting healing of a wide range of maladies.

Literally thousands of studies from around the world have shown that mental and emotional stress and unease are at root of many seemingly physical biological disorders, and that the auto-immune system is bolstered by an upbeat mental attitude. And in our own lives we can all confirm that the basic sign that we have recovered from some illness is that we are at peace again, that we feel joy again. Doesn't it make common sense to *practice* and magnify peace and joy as a preventative measure?

The Natural Preventative Medicine

When we ask the questions, *Am I enjoying riding this thought train, yes or no*? Or *am I at peace with this thought train, these stories, yes or no?* we are engaging in preventive medicine. Or more accurately, when we choose to actually enjoy our trains of thought, or be at peace with our stories, we are then engaging in preventive medicine, as well as adopting curative remedies. (If we ask the questions and don't *act* on the answer by actually changing what we're thinking, or changing our attitude about what we're thinking, then we are simply "suffering more intelligently," as Dr. Almayrac often pointed out.)

We aren't bringing any new revelations here. The fact that most kids are healthy most of the time and that most kids are happy most of the time are two facts that are seldom put together. Of course we all, no matter our age, have our biological/physiological struggles, causes and effects, but the line between mental and emotional and biological and physiological--which is which?—is a very thin and very fuzzy line. Amrit Goswami, physics professor at the University of Oregon and world renowned authority on quantum physics wrote a book entitled *The Self Aware Universe,* suggesting that, when we look very, very closely at the smallest or largest "pieces" of the universe, we find the presence of awareness, we find intelligence itself.

When we practice the Freedom Game or the Peace Game, when we take the time to enjoy the moment, be at peace with ourselves and those around us, we are quietly aligning ourselves with the universe, and simultaneously bringing ourselves back into health and wholeness.

But then the trash needs to be taken out, or the garage cleaned. The boss wants that report by Monday. The laundry's piling up. Is there an easy way to bring all of this talk about "universal alignment" out of the mental and ethereal realms--or just out of book theory--into our day-world experience? What would we pay to be able to make this discussion very practical, very immediate, and bring it all home? If we could bring all of this discussion together, and do it regularly, come back into the moment, for say, just five or six bucks,, would we spend the cash?

Ahh, we've set the stage for the third game. Perfect timing!

Chapter 10

Game Three: The Five-Dollar Timer

Slow Down Time and Tame Promiscuous Attention

"The only reason for time is so that everything doesn't happen at once." --Albert Einstein

Pot and Distorted Time

One of the more curious and mostly pleasurable side effects of pot is the sense of a distortion of time. "Distorted" only from our ordinary daily sense of *hurry-hurry-hurry.* Most of us may in fact actually "live" with a distorted--*hurry hurry hurry*--sense of time. Thus, pot can bring us back to a clearer, more natural view of reality! Life itself is not in a hurry!

When smoking weed we often have a perception that time has slowed down, or, in its most delicious moments, that we have moved into a "timeless" zone or state of consciousness.

The third *Potless Pot High* game, which I accidentally stumbled upon through my personal and professional interest in managing attention, likewise slows down time. The *timer game* brings the first two games--where we practice peace and joy--into practical, time/space frameworks. The timer offers a tangible, literally hands-on approach to playing with time (and joy and peace) during our daily round of affairs.

Attention and the Roots of Addiction

To put this game in context, we need to first talk a little more about attention itself because the timer game is in essence a simple and powerful way of playing with our attention. More precisely, the timer allows us to *frame* our attention, with the result that time slows down and life gets big! Not only big, but easy. (A bit like smoking pot, yes?)

As previously mentioned, I stumbled upon the timer game after many years of working in the addictions field with many hundreds of people--in the early years, some of them sentenced to come see me, and later (thank goodness) most of them coming voluntarily. I've also worked closely with the addictions of various of my friends and family and, of course, with my own addictions, which were sometimes silly and sometimes serious.

Here in my silver haired years I've come to understand that **every addiction is at root an addiction of attention**. It's our *attention* that first gets addicted, whether it be to gambling, sex, drugs, alcohol, movies, buying new shoes or running. After our *attention* becomes habituated (gets hooked), then our bodies join the game. This is a subtle yet powerful insight not yet widely emphasized in treatment of addictions. Since it is our *attention* that first becomes addicted, shouldn't we first be working to *free* our attention? When our attention is free, the body will happily follow!

Attention is a magical energy. It's life's basic energy. One of its qualities: **Whatever we put our attention on, *grows*.** Whether it be something positive or something negative, either way, whatever we put our attention on will start to grow. When we have found some rest (of our attention) or relief (of our attention) in some activity, or person or place or thing, we want to return there. Caring for our attention is a little like caring for a squirming, restless two year old—an ongoing, mandatory project. What a relief, then, when we find some game, or toy or safe environment that will keep the squirming two year old occupied for a while.

Unlike a two year old, however, our mature attention is willing to return to the same game, the same toy, time and again. And we let it, because we are finding a little rest from its constant prowl, its ceaseless demands. This is the root of addiction.

I was once giving a presentation on addiction, attention and the *Potless* games to the professional staff of our local Health District where I worked. I knew that one of the senior executives had a not-so-secret fondness for gambling. At one point in the presentation, I asked the group--about seventy people--how many of them could tell me how many gambling casinos were in a 70 mile radius.

A certain blankness fell over most of their faces, while the executive's face lit up like a slot machine. I could have as easily asked how many high-end shoe stores are in town (one of the tech ladies has a "new shoes" compulsion) or chocolate shops or premier coffee stalls. Each of these activities can be addictive because this is where various people have learned to enjoy themselves, or "rest their attention." When such activities are mentioned, those people's attention immediately perks up, their circuits are connected, like the family dog hearing the refrigerator open.

Attention is Promiscuous

Here's how it works: where our attention has found rest, has found even a bit of peace or joy, if even for a moment, if only a little bit, it wants to return there. Here's why: For most of us, our attention is almost uncontrollably promiscuous. We want it to be monogamous, and pretend that it is so, but our attention gets caught first here then there and while it's in the middle of "there" something else catches it and off it goes.

For example, I start to do the dishes but my attention gets caught by a magazine on the counter. I decide to glance through it quickly but as I do so the car advertisement reminds me I needed to call cousin Louie. So I put the magazine down to go look up Louie's phone number but then suddenly remember that in his last e-mail Louie announced he'd changed his phone number. So now to call

Louie I need to quickly look at his last e-mail, so I go to my computer, open my e-mail and then . . .

Yea, right. An hour and half later I hear a voice from the other room. "Honey, remember it's your night to do the dishes." Not that I didn't think about doing the dishes during that hour and a half, but something else had caught my attention, was more fun, "just for a minute."

First here, then there and everywhere, **our attention is always on the move. We'd like to give it a rest.** So maybe we turn on the television, or the computer game, or have a smoke. Or a bag of chips, something to eat. Maybe a hit of smack. Or a crossword puzzle. And when we do, *ahh, yes,* attention, for a brief moment, finds a little rest.

When we find some activity, or relationship, or drug or game in which our attention finds some joy, or even just a little rest, a little peace and relaxation, we tend to go back to it. It feels almost like a survival mechanism. We *need* this rest, this peace. Our attention needs this rest, this peace.

And if on our return we again find a little rest or relief or pleasure--even if it's not as great as what we experienced the first time--that activity or relationship or game or drug will become attractive to our attention, because our attention has found at least a little rest. And when we put our attention on that activity or relationship or game or drug. **attention itself "grows" that activity into our lives,** to a point we become identified with it, e.g. addicted to it.

Taking Billboards Personally

Okay, that's a brief overview of attention and the roots of addiction. Let's move on to our third game—the timer game--with this caveat: *this game can be addictive*! I know this from personal experience. I'm a timer junkie!

Again, some background about how I got hooked. One of my early "eureka!" moments regarding the place and power of attention, after seeing how it functions in the addiction process, was while reading Michael Goldhaber's seminal essay, *"The Attention Economy, The Natural Economy of the Net*." Reading his essay, I was reminded (again) how very valuable my attention was—*is*. Hard cash on the barrelhead valuable. Our attention is something so familiar and commonplace that we often overlook its value. But corporations are spending millions and millions of dollars *every day* to capture our own, normal every-day attention.

After reading Goldhaber's essay, I suddenly took the junk mail and billboards, television commercials and spam *personally*. I suddenly realized it was *my* attention that all of these were aimed at capturing. I decided that since there were so many ruthless, unremitting, well-funded campaigns to capture *my* attention, all day, every day, for all manner of things, just to protect myself I needed to build up my "attention muscles."

At the time I was commuting to work most every day to Boulder, Colorado, about forty miles from my home. So I borrowed my wife's kitchen timer with the intention of training myself to "pay attention" during my commute. I was going to *really* pay attention--- out the windshield, and the side windows, and back windows. Look at everything really closely. I was going to train myself to be *really* alert, be very present.

So I started by setting the timer for twenty minutes--- I was going to be *really* alert and present for twenty minutes. Alas, after trying that a couple of times, I woke up to the nature of attention and got real. *"Okay, This time I'm going to try to be really alert for just two minutes."*

Attention is indeed quite promiscuous.

Nevertheless, this was the start of my playing with the timer in relation to my attention. I discovered it was sort of fun to *really pay attention* for two minutes. With the timer going, when I noticed I was once again lost in some story in my head, I could drop the story and come back to paying attention to the drive. And then, getting bored with that, I realized I could use the timer to put my attention on some particular story, or idea, or train of thought, again say for two minutes or so. When attention wandered to some different story, or jumped on a different train, I would gently bring it back. I found this was do-able if I did it for a short period of time, using the timer.

Timer as a Tool for Framing Attention

In short, I discovered that the five dollar portable kitchen timer is a very efficient tool for "framing" attention. And more precisely, for reclaiming attention, when necessary, from all of the random and promiscuous adventures it tends to engage. And most miraculous of all, I discovered that when I intentionally reclaim my attention, using the timer, that I am able to *rest* my attention, be it on something as mundane as doing the dishes or as profound as how to experience more peace in my life.

I now use the timer a lot, most every day, primarily because it's fun and I enjoy it, but also because I find the timer helps me get the things done that I want to get done, or need to get done, while *keeping my "get-high" mindset* as I'm doing such things.

For example – back to the dishes. I will often look at the dishes and estimate that it will take me, say, twenty minutes to get the job done. So I set the timer for twenty minutes. Then, curiously, when I'm doing the dishes, *I'm just doing the dishes*! I'm not thinking about cousin Louie, or my e-mail, or maybe I should next do the laundry. I find **when I set the timer for such an ordinary task I am much more present, more relaxed, more willing to be *here* in the moment** doing what I'm doing. (Isn't that what pot also helps us do, at least sometimes?)

In business it's called the "cost of opportunity." If I decide I'm going to make widgets, then I have lost the opportunity to make buggy whips. If I decide I'm going to do the dishes, I'm not cleaning the upstairs bathroom. Doesn't mean I won't at some time clean the upstairs bathroom or make buggy whips, but I don't need to put my attention there in *this* moment. I can *rest* my attention on what I'm doing.

Here's an important part of this: Be clear that I'm *not* trying to get the dishes done in twenty minutes. Twenty minutes is just my estimate of how long this task will naturally (easily) take. I am not interested in adding more stress or pressure to my life. *Au contraire.* If it takes me 25 minutes to clean the kitchen, so be it. If I get it done in 15 minutes, that's okay too. **The purpose of using the timer is to frame attention and more precisely to *rest* attention, *free up* attention to *just do the dishes*!**

We make hundreds, even thousands of decisions a day as to what we will do next--take a shower, get dressed, do the dishes, do the taxes, mow the lawn, etc. My discovery was that when I "freeze framed" some of those tasks by using the timer, I slowed down, I was happier, I was more present, (much like when I used to smoke pot!).

To Escape Time, Use A Timer Rather than a Clock

Here's another important piece of this game. I've discovered that actually using a timer is necessary--rather than trying to use a clock. With a clock, I'm forced to constantly check the time. With the timer, I can forget about time!

Curiously, although it seems as though the timer makes us more conscious of time, it's one of the few ways I know of that actually allows us, or more precisely, allows our attention, to *escape* time, to step outside of time. (Again, much like pot, eh?) If we use a clock, we are forced to become clock watchers. Using a timer, we have a willing little servant who does that for us!

Although on the surface this is the most "materialistic" of the games offered here--you actually need to purchase and use a portable timer to play the timer game--I know from experience and with sharing the game with family, friends and clients that the use of a timer often turns out to be a very emotionally and psychologically centering practice. And yes, a somewhat addictive practice.

Once you get caught on this game you will undoubtedly discover hundreds of other personal uses for your timer. However, to get you started, in the next chapter I will share ten different basic uses of the timer that I've discovered and use in my own "get high" practice. I encourage people to approach the timer game as an experiment, testing which ones are fun for them, which ones not, which ones get you high, which ones don't. In the next chapter you'll find my starter pack. As always, the first one's free…

Chapter 11

Ten Uses for a Timer

"The bad news is time flies. The good news is you're the pilot."
---- Michael Althsuler

Okay, here's my "starter kit"--ten uses for the timer. Again, a warning: you start playing with a timer, it can become addictive. (It's so much fun!)

1. One Minute "Letting Go'" meditations

"How beautiful it is to do nothing and then to rest afterwards."
----Spanish proverb

This one's easy. Simply set the timer for one minute, and *do nothing*! For one minute allow yourself to *not* fix any problems. Just rest, be at peace, *enjoy* all the thoughts inside, all the sights outside, all the relationships and lack of relationships. Again, do *nothing* for just one minute. Don't fix any problems.

Just breathe. For one minute, *just be*! If it helps, you might find it useful to use a word or phrase to remind yourself what you're doing here. Simply say to yourself, *"do nothing,"* or *"let go,"* or *"just enjoy,"* or *"just be."*

When you find your attention getting caught on some inner or outer story or condition or worry or duty, return to your phrase, *"do nothing, let go."* After your one minute of doing nothing and letting go, if you feel so moved, you are free to do another minute, and then another. You can do these one minute "let go" meditations anywhere--in the car, or walking, or at work. I have no doubt that after initial feelings of guilt and hesitation (we are seldom if ever encouraged to simply "do nothing") you will quickly find such a practice very, very refreshing--uplifting! (*High making?*)

When working with addictions I have found that this one minute "do nothing, let go" exercise is powerful. (After all, walking away from an addiction is just letting it go, yes?) Most of us are very addicted to being somewhere else in our heads, in the past or the future. This is a nice little game to bring us back to the now.

What's your response to this game? Let it go!

2. Five minute "Huge Project" starters.

"Mountains cannot be surmounted except by winding paths."
--Goethe

We all have huge projects that we *don't* want to start simply because, well, they're huge! We need to clean out the garage, or the attic, start on that woodpile, or that novel, or the taxes from two years ago. But the project is just *too huge* to even begin! We don't have the time or the psychic energy.

Here's some good news: **We don't need to do the Huge Project**. Instead, we can select an easy, simple, quite doable little project. We do that by setting our timer for just five or ten minutes.

For example, a number of years back I had the great American garage—a garage so full that the car stayed in the driveway. I had good excuses of course—both our kids had moved out, and then moved back and then out again, leaving lots of their old and new stuff behind each time. And both my mom and mother-in-law had recently passed on and much of their stuff also ended up in our garage. And then, come to find out, my wife and I also had lots of our own stuff in there. The garage had taken years to get so stuffed. To clean it out was too big of a project.

So I set the timer for five minutes. In that first five minutes I pounded in a nail to hang up the dust pan and another nail right above that for the whisk broom. There. Done. And it was kinda fun. I felt accomplished. The next evening I gave myself ten minutes. And that was fun. And then within a week or so--bold man that I am—I started giving myself 30 minutes. We now park in the garage, and my tools are nicely hung up, and we have shelves. It's organized (sort of)! My wife and I now do the same thing with taxes, and cleaning out the flower beds, and the storage room.

Here's why it works: Often, when we begin to tackle a huge project, the only reason we stop is because we run out of time or get frustrated, not knowing where to put things, or we get tired or called away to do something else. So when we next think about going back to that huge project, we remember running out of time, or getting frustrated or tired. It's only natural that we don't want to go there again.

When we do five or ten or thirty or sixty minutes at a time, (using the timer, not the clock!) we don't get so tired or frustrated. In fact, it's kinda fun! Much like getting high! When we get high we generally don't get tired or frustrated, and it's kinda fun! The timer works wonders for "Huge Projects." It lets us do what we need to do, peaceably, if not joyfully. The timer allows us to get started.

3. Five Minute "Let me think about that.."

"No problem can withstand the assault of sustained thinking." --- Voltaire

We obviously spend much time thinking about many, many things that are very important to us, or just interesting to us—our work, our kids, our parents, our future, our homes—but we generally do such thinking in brief, random, one and two second fits, flashes, jumbled smorgasbords. To give ourselves five minutes—timed—to think about *one particular topic* proves to be very powerful. **We can often get more "thinking" done in five *dedicated* minutes than in a week of random musings.** Five minutes dedicated to thinking about one thing can lead to brilliance!

When I have something I want to think more deeply about, maybe even while I'm out walking, I'll set my timer. When my thoughts wander, as they naturally do, I gently bring them back to the topic at hand. Again, we can become addicted to this process because it often leads to very powerful insights.

A subtle linguistic point: As we'll discuss in a later chapter, when we set the timer to *think* about a particular topic for a particular amount of time (which is regularly done in business focus groups) we aren't actually *thinking* about this topic. In fact, we are suspending our thinking to put our *attention* on this topic. Attention is prior to thinking. Attention generates thinking. It's a subtle point, but useful. "Let me put my attention on that for a minute." It's *attention* that's powerful! Attention leads to insights. When we set the timer to put our *attention* on something for a specified amount of time, we discover the power of attention, and its secrets!

4. **Ten minute "clean-up, pick-up" project frames**.

"There is no daily chore so trivial that it cannot be made important by skipping it two days running." Robert Brault

Yes, the living room needs to be picked up, the bathroom cleaned, the laundry folded and put away. We *always* have such chores! When we give such chores a "time frame," we discover we enjoy the chores more! And thus we get more chores done. Somehow, it's a lot easier to get started on "ten minutes to pick up the living room," than just start on picking up the living room. Whether it's five minutes, ten minutes, twenty or thirty, **making the time frame is the key**.

My wife would often do this with our kids when they were young. "We're going to clean your room for ten minutes." And she would set the timer. It was a game and they enjoyed it (once they actually got into it.) They knew there was an *end* to this chore.

We're all kids at heart, yes? Let's play more games.

5. **Ten minute "waiting to go" project frames**.

"Time is what we want most, but what we use worst."
--- William Penn

Most of us try to do too many things "before going." When we need to leave in twenty minutes, we either don't get started on anything (not enough time) or try to do too much. Making the decision to do something for "ten minutes," (or twenty or five, depending on departure time) allows for smooth transitions, and *enjoyable* productivity. Using a timer here is like having a personal assistant, an attentive stage manager, who sticks her head in the door and says, "curtain time in five minutes!" We get to be the star of the show.

Again, **the timer here is a device that simply allows us to be in the present more easily, more gracefully**. And when used in the hours or minutes before needing to leave, it helps us to stay in the flow, establish a flow. Which is, not coincidentally, what it often feels like when smoking weed. We're resting our attention in the present!

6. **Fifteen minute "hate to do it/ have to do it "project frames**

"The robbed that smiles, steals something from the thief."
-- Shakespeare (Othello)

This is somewhat like the "Big Project" starter, though this is for the more mundane, everyday tasks. The bills do have to be paid, the dog has to be walked. (The kitchen cleaned up!) Putting the timer to such tasks allows us to see *beyond* the tasks--to see where in our day—or morning or evening--these tasks will fit. Obviously, I say "fifteen minutes" but these can be 10 or 20 minute time frames. To repeat: the timer helps us to be in the moment, in the flow, not resisting our lives and the delicious "daily duties" that in fact are life's meat and potatoes!

As mentioned, my wife and I use the timer to prepare our taxes--which for us is one of those "hate to do it/have to do it" chores. (Some people, I understand, love to do their taxes. Such differences are what make the world go around!) For the taxes I set the timer for fifteen minutes. It's surprising what can be accomplished in fifteen minutes--gathering papers, or looking for papers. Looking at bank statements, etc. When done fifteen minutes at a whack, doing taxes ends up kinda fun!

Cleaning closets, or drawers, or sorting laundry likewise become easy chores when they have a time frame, a *timer* frame around them. It's a way of staying high, cruising, not fighting our lives.

7. **Fifteen minute "reach out and touch someone" (some *institution*) frames.**

"Bureaucracy is a giant mechanism operated by pygmies."
--- Honore de Balzac

This one's a bit trickier. At one time I thought I could set my timer to make it easier for me to call Uncle Billy--which I generally hesitated to do because Uncle Billy, living by himself, can get real talky. I discovered that setting a timer for such personal calls doesn't work that well, at least for me. It feels mean and artificial and shallow. It seems that for people we know and love, or for colleagues, friends and neighbors, the timer can get in the way. It feels fake to "frame" our relationships in this way. When we try to put another live human being into our "timer frame," the human gets squished. We humans don't fit into frames like that. (If you figure out a way to do that, let me know!)

Nevertheless, it *does* work for calling the phone company, or the bank or insurance people, or the doctor's office or the stockbroker. Not that we're going to cut them off after fifteen minutes if our business isn't taken care of by that time. But it helps us put the task into a framework, see how it fits in the day. And we don't get so frustrated when we are put on hold, or made to talk to a robot. We can also use the timer for filling out online applications or making online queries about some product or service.

We tend to quietly overestimate or underestimate the amount of time it takes for these affairs. The advantage here is that we bring our inner estimate to the outer mechanism—the timer—and somehow the task becomes more peaceable, and thus more do-able. Timing such outreaching may seem a silly, unnecessary addendum to our day—and sometimes it is. But again, test it out. You will be surprised at how much peace this little timer can bring to daily affairs.

8. Time Your Routine Chores

"Time is an illusion. Lunch time doubly so."
--- Douglas Adams

This is a little different use for the timer. Here we are curious to discover how much time it actually takes to do a particular chore. Again, we're not trying to do it in a particular amount of time. We're just curious about how much time various routine chores actually, naturally, easily take.

For example, we have two bird feeders on the back porch, and one out by the dining room window. Anybody who has bird feeders knows it's a fun idea to begin with, but the feeders do need to be refilled on a regular basis. I confess several months after installing our feeders I started to feel a bit burdened by this repetitive chore. And then one morning I set my timer, assuming it was about a ten minute chore.

Come to find out it takes me less than three minutes! I was very surprised. I had been making it a much bigger chore in my head than it was in real life. I now find it easy to refill the feeders.

Curiously, in the same way, it takes only a little more than four minutes to unload the dishwasher. That's a chore we make bigger in our head than it actually is in real life. And the same goes for sorting the laundry and cleaning the bathroom. Answering e-mail, on the other hand, generally takes much longer than we expect.

Obviously, this is a little different than setting the timer to allow attention to rest on a particular chore, where we aren't concerned about the time it takes to accomplish the chore. Here we want to know how long it *actually* takes to do a chore. Timing it just once is generally enough to release the false sense of time.

Why are we doing this? For fun. And because we're curious. And to make our day go smoother, to enjoy our day more, be more at peace with our day and our regular routines. This is, after all, as we learned in the first two games, the most important thing for ourselves and all those around us!

9. One minute to twenty minute exercises----be they mental, emotional or physical.

"I don't exercise. If God wanted me to bend over he'd have put diamonds on the floor." --- Joan Rivers

Using a timer for physical exercises is one of the more common uses of a timer. Again, it's much easier, more relaxing and efficient to use a timer rather than a clock. For example, if we decide we want to walk for thirty minutes, we can set the timer for 15 minutes and head out. When the timer goes off, we turn back. Or we can decide to do five or ten or twenty minutes of stretching, or breathing exercises, or weight lifting. The timer sets the frame for such physical exercises.

We can also use the timer for mental and emotional 'exercises.' In the next chapter we'll look more closely at prayer and meditation and how either or both might help us stay high, clear and spunky without weed. For now let me just suggest that the timer functions as a wonderful "trainer" for inner mental and emotional exercises. We can indulge ourselves in five or ten minutes thinking about quantum physics, or advanced calculus, memorizing a poem or attempting the Sunday New York Times crossword puzzle. We can decide to be grateful or loving or peaceful for five minutes straight. In brief, the timer helps us to *play* with our inner thoughts and feelings. To have more fun. To explore. To try something we've never done before. Again, as Bob Dylan puts it, "Those not busy being born are busy dying."

A couple of buddies and I have played the game where we see if we can enjoy everything that comes up, within or without, for five minutes straight. Such exercises quickly show us our habitual crankiness. They also show us it's possible to enjoy our lives. Again, that's what the timer is all about.

10. Thirty- sixty- to ninety minute "one time" projects.

"Pleasure in the job puts perfection in the work."
--- Aristotle

My wife and I recently installed a new, shiny light fixture over our dining room table. My own talents and interests would lead me to write a poem about such a project rather than the actual doing of it. Nevertheless, it's something we wanted to do and it needed to be done, so I set the timer for 90 minutes. Again, not that I was trying to get the chore done in 90 minutes. I set the timer so that I would be more patient, more at rest, with the inevitable "hang ups" (so to speak) that come with hanging and wiring a new light fixture.

Some experts suggest that stress comes not so much from what we are *doing*, but from being *interrupted* in what we are doing. When we take on a project such as hanging a chandelier, the "end result"—a hung chandelier—too easily becomes the image for "what we are doing." Therefore, the stubbornness of the old light fixture to release its 30 year grip can be viewed as an *interruption* of the project. My experience is that when I set the timer, what would have once been an interruption is now simply part of the process, *i.e.*, part of the 90 minutes. I don't get so stressed, so cranky. It's as if I've "scheduled time" to deal with the stubborn old fixture that won't come down. In other words, I more easily maintain my peace, my joy.

And this, let us remember--maintaining and enhancing our experience of peace and joy--is the only reason we're playing with the timer in these ways. To have fun, to more deeply experience the richness, the fullness of the immediacy of our lives. Yes, we might find that by playing with the timer we get more things done, we are better organized, we are more persistent in working towards our goals. But these benefits are the gravy of the process. Increased joy and peace are the meat and potatoes.

If we should find times and places where the timer is getting in the way of our peace and joy, what do we do? We quickly abandon it! If it's not fun, let's not do it.

Nevertheless, by "framing" our activities with the timer, we are more likely to stay present, focused, in the flow. But obviously, we don't set the timer for everything we do during the day. That would be neither fun nor practical. So what other ways might we "frame" our day to reinforce our joy, our peace, *i.e.,* to stay high, clear and spunky? Is there something we might do, maybe in the morning and evening (other than shooting smack) that will help keep us high during the day?

Glad you asked. Let's talk a little, in the next chapter, about the "get high" meditation routine.

But before we leave this chapter, for a few "after dinner mints," here are a few more time quotes that I wanted to use in this chapter but couldn't find the right place. So here they are, on their own, just for fun:

Time is the coin of your life. It is the only coin you have, and only you can determine how it will be spent. Be careful lest you let other people spend it for you. - Carl Sandburg

You have to allow a certain amount of time in which you are doing nothing in order to have things occur to you, to let your mind think. --- Mortimer Adler

Until you value yourself, you won't value your time. Until you value your time, you will not do anything with it.
---M. Scott Peck

And best of all for this chapter:
I must govern the clock, not be governed by it.
---Golda Meir

Chapter 12

Game Four:
The *Spontaneous Grin* Meditation Practice

Establishing Basic Routines for the Daily *Get-High*

"One filled with joy preaches without preaching."
--- Mother Teresa

Let's back up a minute (set your timers!) to refresh our memories about what we are doing here, what this book is all about. What we are looking for is some way to get high, clear and spunky without the use of pot. And since we've come this far, we can take it a step further and admit we're actually looking for ways to *stay* high, clear and spunky. And, more specifically, stay easy, natural and free. Stay loving, cruising, *grinning*, from morning 'til night.

Is Such a Goal Reasonable? Doable?

Sure, the goal of grinning "from morning 'til night, all day every day" is a very high bar (so to speak) towards which we are aiming. But why not? We only live once, right? (Well, maybe not. But you know what I mean.) Let's go for the gold. Rumors are afloat that there are many out there who have achieved such a state--grinning with their lives!

In fact, many spiritual traditions, and the seers and the wise ones of these traditions, affirm that this "high state"--this gold state, grinning state--is in truth our *natural* state. This may be why the grinning effects of pot are so attractive to so many people: The high state hints at something very real inside us. Being free, loving and cruising is our *natural* way of being--though as we all know, pot doesn't necessarily always "work" to get us there, to the grins, or keep us there on a consistent basis.

Alas, most people do not ordinarily experience their natural, happy *gold state* throughout their ordinary work days. People not aware of their joy, their peace, has been described as akin to sleeping. In such "waking sleep," we are not conscious of our true nature.

An old story suggests that after the Buddha's enlightenment, he passed a man on the road who was struck by the Buddha's extraordinary radiance and peaceful presence. The man stopped the Buddha and asked, "What are you? Are you a celestial being or a god?"

"No," said the Buddha.

"Well then are you some kind of magician or wizard?"

Again, the Buddha answered "no."

"Are you a man?"

"No."

"Well then what are you?"

"I am awake."*

(*Thanks to Teachings of the Budha.com)

Wakefulness, although very natural, has been a fairly rare state of being amongst us mortals, though in this new millennium it now appears that more and more ordinary folks are simply starting to wake up. (Doesn't that coffee smell good?)

Wake with Joy?

So how do we wake up? How do we reclaim our natural state of being? As you might guess, my first suggestion is that we start by playing the Freedom Game, and/or the Peace Game, all day, every day. Whenever necessary or appropriate we simply ask, "*Do I enjoy riding this thought train, telling these stories,* or *am I at peace with this thought train, these stories, yes or no*?

If and when we are giving our time and energy and importance to thoughts and stories we *don't* enjoy, that are troubling or unhappy for us, we can be sure that we are still sleeping, unaware of our true nature, or at least lightly dozing. A deep sense of peace and joy *always* attends greater wakefulness. (If not, who needs wakefulness?)

Let's be clear: Attending to peace and joy doesn't mean that we don't deal with the wars and the poverty and the violence and injustice that we encounter. Rather, as Einstein said, "We can't solve problems by using the same kind of thinking we used when we created them."

Or, as Gandhi pointed out, again and again, "The means and the ends are the same." If we want to wake up, and bring peace and joy to earth, we need to *start* with peace and joy, even if we have only a glimmer, a sliver of the stuff. That's where we begin: with what we have.

In the Freedom Game we posit that "Enjoying our happiness is the most loving thing we can do for ourselves and all those around us." In the Peace Game we suggest that "Practicing peace of mind is the most practical thing we can do for ourselves and all those around us." I always encourage my clients to not take my word for this. I encourage them to test it out—is it true that enjoying happiness really *is* the most loving thing we can do for ourselves and others? If it's not--then what *is* more loving? Is practicing peace of mind *really* the most practical thing we can do? If not, what's more practical?

Let's assume that we have personally tested these hypotheses and discovered that, at least for ourselves, yes, enjoying our happiness is in fact the most loving thing we can do, and that practicing peace of mind is the most practical activity we can engage in. (Obviously, these two things are not mutually exclusive. It's impossible to enjoy ourselves if we are not, at least for the moment, at peace with ourselves. And peace of mind is in fact quite enjoyable.)

So **if enjoying our happiness and practicing peace of mind are what are most loving and most practical, doesn't it make sense that we should devote at least a little time each day to doing *just this*—to *just* enjoying our happiness, *just* practicing peace**?

Yes, of course, we want to enjoy our happiness and practice peace while we're at the grocery store or having dinner with the family or talking with our clients. These types of activities are what make up our lives. Bringing peace and joy to earth is not a part time gig.

However, my experience has been that in order to practice peace and enjoy my happiness during all the "ordinary" events of my life—*i.e.*, to stay high, clear and spunky throughout the day-- it is very useful for me to set aside at least a little time when I am doing *just this* and nothing else.

And again, how do we practice peace of mind, or enjoy our happiness? By riding thought trains we enjoy to ride and/or telling stories with which we are at peace. But how can we do "just this" and nothing else?

It's obviously going to be easier to do "just this"-- think thoughts we enjoy to think, thoughts with which we are at peace--when we're alone, maybe sitting in a quiet room by ourselves, and maybe even with our eyes closed, just enjoying our thoughts, being at peace with our thoughts. And yes, it's almost always easiest to find a quiet room and time for ourselves first thing in the morning, and/or after work in the evening, or right before we go to a bed.

Hmmm . . . sounds a bit like meditation, doesn't it? (And yes, it also sounds like smoking weed. Our quest, though, is for the *potless* enlightenment!) Let's take it to the next level and suggest that if the thought trains you most enjoy to ride or with which you are most at peace have to do with the Divine, we might call it *prayer* and meditation. Can prayer and meditation be this simple--just thinking thoughts we enjoy to think or with which we are at peace? Why not?

(Here's a little secret: prayers you *enjoy* to pray get to go to the front of the line! Well, okay, there really isn't a line. But prayers we *enjoy* to pray somehow seem to get answered quickest! In fact, the joy itself is part of the answer!)

Simple Prayer and Meditation

Obviously, whole libraries have been written on both prayer and meditation. And what wonderful libraries these be! (I have my own personal version of such libraries.) Yet**, if prayer and meditation don't lead to greater peace and more joy, why on earth would we want to engage such practices**? In fact, if they don't lead to peace, to joy, to hell with them! We already have way too many practices—both spiritual and secular--that do *not* lead to peace and happiness.

And if that *is* where these practices are leading--to more peace and more joy--isn't it both wise and fair to go *directly* there? And how do we go *directly* there? Duh. By thinking thoughts we enjoy to think and thoughts with which we are at peace. *Any* thoughts.

As is true for many in my generation, I have been led over many decades to play with, experiment with, love and fight with many hundreds of versions of prayer and meditation, some silly, some profound. I have had the good fortune to be exposed to teachers and techniques and practices from literally every tradition, beginning with what I was taught as a child in Sunday school. What a smorgasbord of spiritual practices we have available in these modern times!

In my maturity, I am comfortable with the notion that when any of these practices lead to the immediate, momentary experience of tangible peace and joy, I will use them, love and honor them. But when such practices lead, as they often do, to boredom, or to more pain or self-doubt or alienation from myself, from family and friends, I have no patience or tolerance for them. And I don't engage some technique because it promises some kind of salvation or enlightenment further down the road. Life's too short. Peace and joy are available right here, right now. Why wait?

In this season of my life, my morning meditation practice is quite simple. Four or five or six days out of seven, (sometimes more, seldom less) I rise either before the sun comes up or as it's coming up. This is not because I'm disciplined, but rather simply because in this season of my life I seem to enjoy my morning routines more than the late-night entertainments with which I was once enamored. In other words, I *enjoy* what I do in the early mornings, so I find it easy to wake up early!

Upon rising, after performing natural old guy functions and after brushing my teeth, but still in my shorts, before coffee or breakfast or news, I'll go to my den, pull a shawl around my shoulders for warmth, and then, for the next twenty to sixty minutes or so, indulge myself in simply being at peace, enjoying the moment, riding whatever thought trains I enjoy to ride, thought trains with which I am at peace. That's it! That's how uncomplicated my current morning meditation and prayer practice happens to be. I repeat: This is *not* a discipline, it's an *indulgence,* as was pot smoking at one time.

Seven Minute Meditations

For many years, prior to my current simplified practice, I enjoyed to use my timer to focus these early morning meditations into seven minute increments. I would set my timer for seven minutes so it automatically returned to seven minutes without my needing to reset it.

One reason I used a series of seven minute meditations was because in numerological lore the number seven signifies "completeness," and because seven resonates with the tradition in which I was raised. Mostly, however, it was because seven minutes was about as long as I could comfortably keep my attention on just one train of thought or story. (I started out with two minutes, and worked my way up.)

Generally, my first seven minute meditation was to put my attention on the phrase, *"This is the day the Lord hath made—Let us rejoice and be glad in it."* Why did I put my attention on this thought, this story? Simply because I personally find this train of thought to be both a fun and peaceable train to ride, first thing in the morning. If you don't find it to be so, for pity's sake don't use it. **Find a train of thought you *do* enjoy to ride, and focus on it, first thing in the morning**.

When we put our attention on a single sentence--any sentence, be it from scripture or a favorite mystery book--for a whole seven minutes, (bringing attention back to the sentence when it wanders, which it naturally does) the sentence inevitably reveals its deeper significances. Some mornings when I put my attention on "This is the day the Lord hath made—Let us rejoice and be glad in it," my attention might get caught on just the first words, "This is the day." I might start to wonder, what does "this day" actually mean? Yes, it's one revolution of the earth spinning on its axis. But the earth is revolving around the sun and the sun is revolving around the center of the galaxy, which itself is whirling in space. "Day" suddenly takes me to a very expanded place. This one word can bring a grin to my morning sitting.

Other days I might wonder what "Lord" means. Is it like the Christian tradition, where it means Jesus? Or the Jewish tradition, where it means Jehovah? Or in the Hindu tradition, where it can mean Krishna, Shiva, Vishnu or Rama? From the Latin I know that "Lord" means "Law." Maybe I'll just let my mind ponder, for a bit, what, or who, is the law, the lord, that "made the day"? Quantum forces perhaps? Or the law of love? This, too, often brings a grin.

And still other days my attention might be caught on "rejoice." Re-joy? I *joyed* once and now I re-joy? Or I might revise it a bit: "Today's peace (or today's joy or today's being) is the peace the Lord hath made . . ." Again, **I feel**

very free in my morning mediations to think what I enjoy to think, wherever my joy should lead me. After all, that's the point. There are no "wrong' ways to enjoy my thinking, or to be at peace with my stories.

And then my timer goes off and I generally drop that particular thought or story and go on to something else, *anything* else. Or I might enjoy to do that same thought for another seven minutes.

Although my first focus tended to stay the same for many years (*This is the day the Lord hath made—Let us rejoice and be glad in it*) where I went from there in the next seven minutes seemed to change, maybe not daily, but weekly, depending on what I was reading or where yesterday's meditation took me. For many years I played with "just being." I would "just be" for seven minutes. Or maybe I'd look at *who is meditating*? Turn my attention around to look at the meditator. (The meditator tends to disappear when we look too closely!) Or maybe I'll "just chill" for seven minutes. Or "just love," or "drop all stories" for seven minutes.

I'm intentionally glossing over the specific *content* of my own particular daily meditations because the content is not as important as the principle--*enjoying* our thoughts, being at peace with our thoughts. I've had seasons when the content of my morning meditations was very much "prayerful," perhaps focused on family members or work circumstances or national or international tragedies or challenges. Other seasons I've played with the chakra system, or the subtle domains, or traveled the astral regions, and dialogued with the inhabitants therein.

As mentioned, here in my maturity, my meditations are much simpler. My immediate experience of joy and peace is the only standards by which I judge whether to take up—or continue--a particular practice, a particular train of thought or inquiry. **I know a meditation has been successful if it elicits a spontaneous grin**. And if I actually chuckle out loud–which I sometimes do sitting there by myself in the quiet of the first light--I know it's been a *very* good meditation.

I would generally do at least three seven minute meditations, one after the other, in the morning. Sometimes it went on much longer--where I would do five, six, ten or more seven minute meditations. Again, these morning practices are truly not a discipline so much as they are an indulgence!

Even though I find meditation to be a wonderful indulgence, hard science shows that those who meditate for a bit every day—or at least every couple of days-- experience profound benefits from such a practice. Those who meditate sleep better, have lower blood pressure, need less sleep. Meditation tends to reduce symptoms of asthma, "thicken" the gray matter of the brain (making one more intelligent!) and even slow down the aging process. Scientists have documented that meditation is a good thing.

Let's take it a step further and bring it back to our quest for the potless pot high. An article in *Psychology Today* reported, "The brain waves of meditators show why they're healthier. Neuroscientists have found that meditators shift their brain activity to different areas of the cortex—brain waves in the stress-prone frontal cortex move to the calmer left frontal cortex**. In other words, they were calmer and happier than before**."(For a fun read see the article at: http://www.psychologytoday.com/articles/200304/the-benefits-meditation).

"Different areas of the cortex" Doesn't that sound familiar to the marijuana research and the effects of marijuana on the brain that we discussed in earlier chapters?

I know there are teachers who might disagree, some quite strongly, with my simple form or instruction for meditation—*just enjoy your thoughts for a while, be at peace with your thoughts for a while*. After all, thousands of years of meditation practice have led to very intricate "instructions" in all manner of meditation. For example, I've glossed over breathing, which is traditionally very central to most meditation practices. (So okay—just *enjoy* your damned breathing, for pity's sake, be at peace with your breathing.

Count your breaths if you enjoy to do that. Now--we've taken care of breathing!)

Some teachers will insist that much work, much discipline and detailed guidance is necessary while learning to meditate, to concentrate (or de-concentrate), to "break through" the deep patterns of resistance we carry around with us, some of which are even hard-wired in the body. Some teachers insist on long retreats devoted to meditation, starting with simple practices and moving into "conquering" very complex mental and emotional patterns, koans or "mandalas." I even heard one traditional Zen teacher suggest one would need a minimum of ten years full-time daily practice before the first signs of awakening will appear. To suggest something less is misguidance at best, the teacher said, heresy or blasphemy at worst.

So it goes. Many of us experienced what felt to us like the "first signs of enlightenment" after a smoking a bowl of righteous herb. That doesn't take ten years. It takes about a minute.

So okay, some folks will regard what I write here as a blasphemous heresy. I'm not frightened by such a label. I'm simply relating my own direct experience. I do deeply honor all the long traditions of prayer and meditation, and have personally gained much insight and understanding from engaging many, many practices from various traditions. Nevertheless, I stick with my story: **let's go straight to the joy, straight to the peace**. Why not? And isn't this what we are trying to do, and often succeeding, with pot?

The means and the ends are always the same. If you enjoy to do a 30 day silent retreat in a freezing Himalayan cave, go for it! Ten years in a monastery? I bow to you. However, if you assume that being miserable during a 30 day retreat will somehow lead to peace, I know that after such a retreat you will then assume you need another 60 or 90 days, or maybe sign up for the ten year stint to find your peace. Again: **the means and the ends are the same**!

Back to simple meditation: If enjoying our happiness really *is* the most loving thing we can do for ourselves and all those around us, and if practicing peace of mind *is* the most practical thing we can do, doesn't it make sense to regularly devote some time to doing *just this* at points throughout the day? Shouldn't we devote some time to do what is most important in our lives?

And again, I find that the timer is a wonderful aid (though not a necessity) in doing *just this*. For example, when I'm out walking by myself, I will do "walking meditations," where I set the timer--be it for three minutes or five or seven minutes--and again put my attention on some train of thought, concept or insight that I enjoy. They might be the same trains of thought or concepts that I use in my morning meditations, or something completely new. Either way, it's a "walking meditation." What a treat to give myself such joy, such peace--"just this"--during the day.

And then in the evenings, most often right before bed, I again take a few moments, generally twenty minutes or so, to meditate, to transition, let all the busy, busyness of the day settle down, remember again what is most important. I'm amazed at how much better I sleep when I indulge in such a "before bed" meditation.

Early evening meditations are not as common or regular for me now as they once were. (Yes, I did do Transcendental Meditation at one time in my life.) But again-- like going to the movies or the bingo parlor--mediation is an indulgence, a fun thing to do in itself, not a discipline leading to something other.

It *is* possible to be at ease, to grin, feel good about life all day--or at least almost all day—every day. Kids do it naturally. Why should we grown-ups be deprived of such a happy lifestyle? Although we are already naturally happy, naturally at ease, our culture encourages us--even trains us--that we have to "achieve" such happiness, such peace through outer accomplishments. We are encouraged to get a better job, a better home, a better car, a new spouse; we are encouraged to lose ten or twenty pounds and then get the crabgrass out of the lawn--*then* we'll be happy, for a minute or two. And if these things don't work to bring happiness, try drugs, sex and rock and roll, or options on the currency exchange. *These* should make us happy!

Let's be clear here: There's nothing wrong with a better job, a better car, a new spouse, losing twenty pounds or enjoying drugs, sex and rock and roll. Nothing wrong with options on the currency exchange unless our happiness *depends* on such things. When our happiness or peace depends on such outer events or substances, that's when we get ourselves into trouble.

Curiously, my experience is that when we take up the practice of joy, the practice of peace, as a daily *indulgence,* as the *means* rather than the ends, the universe seems to smile on such practices and these other outer outcomes seem to occur more regularly. We end up in the right job, or with the right mate, the right people at the right time. Practicing our joy, our peace, leads us more often to "accidentally" be in the right place at the right time. Our lives gracefully, effortlessly start to *work,* at all levels. This, of course, leads to more and more grins!

So then, of course, the question arises, if we just smoke weed all day long don't we also generate lots of grins. Isn't smoking weed "taking time" to be happy, to be peaceful? What's the difference between playing these Potless games and playing the weed-propelled games? It's a worthy question. To explore such a question, we'll need another chapter.

Chapter 13:

Is the *Potless Pot High* Exactly Like Pot (No.)
Will I Get *Higher* Than I Do with Pot? (Yes)

"If you ever reach total enlightenment while drinking beer, I bet it makes beer shoot out your nose." --- Jack Handy

So the question arises (for some), "If I come home from work and meditate, rather than smoke a bowl, will it be the same?"

No, sorry to say, or happy to say, (depending on your frame). It will be similar, but not exactly the same experience.

Again, as we observed in the first chapter, the games of the *Potless Pot High* generally don't give you a sudden head-rush, a sudden brain melt the way pot can do. It's obviously not as dramatic. And there are other small differences between the two high states, as well as similarities.

Let's focus for a moment on just a single meditation. Let's say we come home from a long day's work and take a few minutes to meditate. As with pot, we will probably experience a welcome release, maybe a spontaneous deep breath, as our brain's alpha waves take prominence over beta, resulting in a state of "relaxed alertness." As with pot, during our meditation our brains will probably begin consciously processing, if not from totally different areas than at least from additional areas of the brain. We will experience what physicists refer to as greater "coherence," where the various parts of the brain are now all playing from the same musical score, rather than from varying scores.

With an evening meditation, as with pot, we will likely find ourselves standing back a bit from the day's intensities, not so caught up with the stresses and concerns of the day immediately past. We will relax, maybe even grin. In these ways pot and meditation are very similar. Either can be a quite righteous change from the day's stresses and strains.

The *difference* between smoking an evening bowl (depending on the quality of pot) and doing an evening meditation (depending on the type of mediation) is that pot is generally going to be much more visceral, more intense, more immediate. The heart rate, for example, speeds up after first smoking pot, but will generally slow down after meditation. And the switch from *where* the brain is processing and *how* the brain is processing is much more exaggerated after smoking a bowl than after meditating Thus, again as mentioned in the first chapter, with pot we generally experience a first head rush, which, especially for long term smokers, both signals and allows an immediate and generally uplifting change in perception and sensory input.

With pot these physiological changes are always more immediate, more dramatic and thus more obvious than with the more subtle changes which result from meditation. So when we're looking for an amusement park, roller coaster type of experience-- which many of us do on occasion-- pot will outperform meditation almost every time. That's just the way it is. On the other hand…

All Day Pot vs. All Day Meditation

If we've been smoking pot all day, beginning with our breakfast bowl, and then again before lunch and then maybe as an afternoon pick-me up and then again as a little something with which to watch the sun go down, then our "evening bowl" is, alas, going to be something akin to a speed bump--giving us a little momentary elevation and then *same ol' same; ol'*. In fact, it doesn't even have to be all day. If smoking weed is what we do every night, the high is not going to be as intense or satisfying--or maybe even as functional (grin inducing)—as it otherwise might be. (Duh.) After a full day (or a week or a month) of smoking weed, our brain tends to be somewhat soggy, foggy, wet noodle-like, yes? It's time to go take a nap.

On the other hand, if we've been meditating all day, maybe beginning with a sun-up tune-up, and then maybe a mid-morning pull back, release of tension, and then maybe again practicing our grins on an afternoon's brief walk--if meditation has been our day-life practice, (*indulgence*!) then it is quite likely that our evening meditation will lead us to being even higher, clearer, spunkier than we've been all day! Which is good news, because we've *already* experienced being high, clear and spunky most of the day.

And if, between our meditations, we've also been playing the Freedom and Peace Games—intentionally, consciously riding only the thought trains that we enjoy, or thought trains with which we are at peace--and maybe we also used the timer to help with our daily transitions from one project to another, continually bringing our attention back to the now *(i.e.,* bringing attention back to reality)--if this has been our practice, we might even *forget* to meditate in the evening simply because we're already cruising! (Just like we used to forget to smoke the other half of the doobie because we're already plenty high!)

We forget to meditate because we're already cruising: Ahh, the Potless Pot High, the weedless enlightenment.

Okay, yes, this may be an exaggeration of the wonders that these games afford. On the other hand . . .

Let me back up and say it again: This is *not* a *recovery* book. Yes, of course, I'm hoping to open some new doors for some of our tribe, or at least point out some doors through which pot smokers and ex-pot smokers and curious onlookers might find some new (higher, clearer, spunkier) adventures awaiting, and through which they might tap into their own (natural ever-present) peace and joy.

For me, sharing these games is as if I've found a pub with giggling bar maids offering free beer and nachos. I want to slip out quick and phone my mates with my happy discovery!

Still, it is clear to me that my own interest in getting high, clear and spunky came about because that was my first experience with pot (and, okay, yes, second and third) just as it has been the experience of millions of others. When we are brave enough to admit to the positive experience of the marijuana high, and thus its natural attraction, only then are we ready to investigate more honestly, more deeply, *exactly* what the pot experience is giving us--what is righteous about it and what is not so righteous about it. And then we'll see if we can separate the wheat from the chaff.

Higher, Clearer, Spunkier

Looking back, I see that I moved away from regular weed use mostly because I wanted to get higher, clearer, spunkier, or more precisely, I wanted to *stay* higher, clearer, spunkier. And yes, I had seasons where I explored whether other substances might do the trick. The main problem, as mentioned in the first chapter, not only with pot but also all the other "recreational" substances, is that we keep coming down. (This is *not* the "main problem" that we hear about or focus on in rehab!)

One distinguishing feature of this "main problem"--the problem of continually coming down after getting high--is that we keep coming down to the *same place*, or something close to the same place. Yes, of course, with pot, over time, we often change and mellow a bit and get a wider view of ourselves and of the world. (With coke or smack or some of the other substances that is *not* necessarily the case.)

With pot, at a certain point, the changes slow down dramatically, and the view gets cloudy. And for some long–time pot heads, the new changes experienced are not even forward moving but rather, we start going in reverse!

Are We Drowning?

This whole phenomenon of coming down to the same place reminds me of an experience I had when I was a young boy, not yet knowing how to swim, when my grandparents took us to the Glenwood Springs swimming pool—the largest outdoor hot springs in the world. It was wonderful. My brothers and I were playing in the shallow end.

Close to the shallow end they had a slide that the big kids were going down. Back in those days it was just a simple slide—climb the ladder, slide straight down, just like on the playground. I really wanted to go down that slide so I studied the situation. It seemed to me that the kids were landing not far from the edge of the pool. I thought that maybe I could go off the slide, then when I hit the water go down to the bottom, push myself off at an angle back toward the edge. I figured it would take me two or three push-offs from the bottom to make my way back to the edge. Sounds like a plan, yes?

So I climbed the ladder, went off the slide--*splash*! It was wonderful. I then sunk to the bottom. And pushed myself off, per my plan. I surfaced, got my bearings, went back down and pushed off again. At my second surfacing I heard my grandmother screaming, from the other side of the pool, "*Get him! get him! get him*! "And saw the lifeguard, eyes wide, crouched on his lifeguard stand, staring at me. Down I went again.

Pushed off, came back up, probably in pretty much the same place I'd been before, though that wasn't obvious to my young eyes. What was obvious was the lifeguard in the air (the image is still with me) diving off his stand in my direction. By the time I came back up the third time, he was there, and had his arm around me, taking me back to shore. So much for my plan.

All these years later I still remember that my first private thought was something like, "Shucks, I'll only get to go down the slide one time." Disappointment that I didn't get to try out my theory. (It might have worked!) I'd learned to be a polite boy, however, and on our way back to the pool's edge I told the lifeguard, "I guess I'll never try that again" (even though I wanted to.) I was quite calm.

And of course, my grandmother (may she rest in peace) was not calm at all and made me promise the same thing--not to go down the slide again. Soon after, my parents enrolled us in swimming lessons.

Let's recap: We smoke pot simply because we're wanting a little buzz, to find a little pleasure, some peace. We want to escape the wars, end the suffering, if only for a bit. We want to enjoy ourselves, enjoy our lives--we want to go off the slide, or go up the slide! We want an adventure. And it *works*, for a little bit.

But we keep coming down. And at some point, it may even feel like we're drowning. Or maybe just going up and down in the same damned place.

Yes, of course, sometimes the splash is wonderful, refreshing, something quite different from yesterday's splash. But we still get a sense that we're just splashing around. And we keep coming down. This *doesn't* happen with the Potless Pot High.

Steadily Higher, Spunkier

Or more accurately, the going up and coming down doesn't happen in the same way. From my experience we are *always* going to have our ups and downs--physically, mentally, emotionally, relationally. That's just life on planet earth. In fact, I'm convinced that at some point physicists will discover that earth itself has "heavy gravity" days and "light gravity" days. Some days we're heavier--seems as though *everybody* is heavier. And some days we're lighter. Some days we're up. Some days we're down.

Here's the deal: With the Potless Pot High, unlike with pot, our ups are *cumulative*. Our high from yesterday helps us be higher today. And our high today helps us get higher tomorrow. When we practice riding only those thought trains we enjoy to ride, practice being at peace with our thoughts and our stories, practice hanging out in our ease, we get better at it. My experience with the Potless games is that we *stay* high—stay easy, grinning-- for longer periods of time and when we do come down, get low, it's for shorter periods of time. That's righteous herb, yes? What would we pay for stuff that makes us higher, clearer and spunkier the more we do it?

Again, *"hey friends, good news--- free beer and giggly bar maids!"*

Pot-Induced Attention Deficit?

Here's another difference between smoking weed and playing the Potless games: As we know, after smoking weed our attention is free to roam all over the galaxies. This is one of the attractions.

However, with such free-rambling, free-roaming attention we tend to forget what we were just doing a moment ago, or we get tired and bored with what we were just doing, or what we were doing last night, so we start something new.

Almost every pot smoker knows the bane of a thousand half-completed projects. This is true of non-pot smokers too, of course. (After all, a project is, by definition, something not yet complete.) Let's admit, however, that smoking pot exaggerates this tendency.

When we are more at ease with the inner territory—which happens when we take up the challenge of enjoying our thoughts, being at peace with our thoughts, from morning to night, via the games already outlined--when we are more at ease with the inner territory--we're naturally more at ease with the outer territory. We discover that our happiness, our peace does not *depend* so much on the circumstances of the outer territory, or more particularly, the outer project.

Thus we don't have to keep moving from one project to another in an attempt to maintain our joy, our peace. We find ourselves more *at ease* in doing the ordinary tasks of washing the dishes, or cleaning out the flowerbeds or going through old boxes of papers. We are happy to take up the next step of last night's project because our happiness does not *depend* on the project. **We bring our happiness *to* the project; we don't derive our happiness *from* the project.** Thus more of our projects get completed.

I hear arguments from the peanut gallery: "No, when I'm stoned I *do* bring my happiness to the project. Getting stoned helps me to get more projects done."

And yes, granted, I do have several stoner friends who live in very tidy spaces and who are consistently productive, not only in their personal lives, but also their wider social and economic lives. So it goes. I love 'em. On the other hand . . .

Let's admit, these folks are the exception rather than the rule. Just as there are "high functioning" alcoholics--exceptions to the rule--we have high functioning stoners. The human organism is a mysterious and wonderfully "un-categorize-able" event. Although we may have spurts of genius (or what *feels* like genius)and productivity while stoned, in general the results are much fuzzier, more relaxed, less productive, generally a bit messier.

Let's be clear here: In a culture where "being productive" is assumed to be the most important thing we can do, indeed, the *only* worthy thing we can do, it may be useful, indeed, even life-saving to step back from such assumptions during some seasons of our lives, re-examine the whole notion. **It is quite obvious that greater productivity does not always or even regularly lead to greater over-all happiness, peace or love**. Indeed, the drive for more productivity can easily diminish these more life nurturing experiences.

On the other hand . . .

My experience is that **more happiness, peace and love do indeed lead to more productivity**. Yet more productivity is a *by-product* of these life-nourishing qualities and not the basic intent. Peace, joy, love are sufficient unto themselves. (Again, "I know it's true," as my wife once said. "But it just sounds so corny!")

We don't need a *reason* to be peaceful, joyful, loving. These qualities are what make up our basic human nature. When we once again get in touch with our basic nature, we find ourselves spontaneously engaged more productively with the nature around us!

Smoking weed has become so popular because it does give us a *hint* of our basic human nature—more relaxed, peaceable, loving. But it doesn't allow us to *live* there. (We keep coming down.) Thus, these weedless games.

In the next chapter we will look at how we can spontaneously share these games with our family and friends and co-workers, and how such sharing magnifies their results. After all, if we're going to bring more peace, joy and love to earth (as corny as it sounds) we have to start with the earth we know!

Chapter 14

Share a (Natural) Doobie with Your Kids, Your Folks and Friends

How and Why the Potless Pot High
Gets Better When Shared with Others

"A happy family is but an earlier heaven."
---- George Bernard Shaw

When I first learned the freedom game from Dr. Almayrac, I was primed. In addition to exploring, with most of my 1960's generation, all the mostly forbidden ways of enjoying ourselves and each other, I had also studied with various teachers from many traditions, both east and west, who had prepared me, knowingly or not, for this simple game, for taking up the "discipline" of joy.

I was very grateful for Dr. Almayrac's genius in simplifying the east/west traditions into such a quick and useful process. (*Do I enjoy riding this thought train, yes or no? If it's not an immediate and spontaneous yes, it's a no*).

Teenage Girls and Happiness?

"But surely, you can't teach, say, a thirteen year old girl that enjoying her happiness is the most important thing for her and for everybody else," I once argued with Dr. Almayrac. "Wouldn't that just give her permission to *party, party, party,* bring on the drugs sex and rock and roll?" I was referring to the fact that in our culture, "enjoying our happiness" is most often translated as "stimulating our senses."

Dr. Almayrac, the father of five children, laughed and quickly set me straight. "Oh no, a thirteen year old girl needs this game most of all," he said. "When she learns that her own joy is already present and is very valuable and necessary, and that she accesses her joy by *what she is thinking,* then she knows **her happiness does not depend on some boy or some group.** She can still enjoy the boys, and enjoy the groups, but she knows her real happiness, not the counterfeit. Then she gets just the right dose (of drugs, sex and rock and roll) and knows when she is not following her true self."

And Dr. Almayrac practiced what he preached. I was almost stunned at the depth of trust he had in his children's joy. "If you don't enjoy to go to school," he would tell his eighth grade son. "Don't go." But his son had learned to love school, enjoyed school immensely and even on days when he was not feeling well, and might stay home, he went.

The Nunnery and College Happiness

In my own family life, when I was first learning the Freedom Game, our daughter was in her second year of college, living in a house close to campus with three roommates, two girls and a boy. As a dad, I suspect there are people and things that daughters are sometimes involved with that dads just as well need not know about. But I was not naïve. In her high school days, in response to some of the friends and activities she was involved with, I had encouraged her (as dads are wont to do) to consider joining the nunnery. "Yeah right, dad."

So although there was a young man living with the three ladies, I assumed it was a "Three's Company" type of arrangement. I hadn't realized anything was going on between our daughter and this fellow until one day the young fellow's stuff was thrown out on the lawn in the rain. Our daughter's doing. "**I am woman. Hear me roar**!"

To briefly encapsulate a tumultuous season, the other two roommates eventually sided with the fellow in this spat. Our daughter, much shaken, not only moved out of their shared house but also dropped out of college and moved back home with the folks. In counseling work, we used to call this a "bottoms out" season.

This was when Dr. Almayrac was giving talks around the area, and had even stayed in our home several times. Our daughter, a very high-level, naturally self-aware lady in her own right (if I may say so) immediately took to the game. "Yes, enjoying my happiness *is* the most loving thing I can do for myself and for everybody else, and yes, I *can* process my thoughts this way."

She learned the Freedom Game and began practicing it immediately. The transition into the next season of her life was relatively smooth. She changed schools, and majors, found new friends, over the next few years received her degree, with high honors. Now, fifteen years later, she is happily married, with a professional job she loves and is the mother of a happy 10-year old. Looking back on this time when she learned the Freedom Game, she says, "**It was like a light came on in my life. I finally had permission to be myself, to be who I really wanted to be**."

Our son and his wife (also bright, high-functioning self-aware folks, if I do say so) have been deeply involved in their church. They were at first a bit hesitant about the Freedom Game, wondering how it fit in with their faith. I reminded them that when Jesus was in the garden, and the goons were about to come and take him away, his guys asked him, "Why are you doing this? What is this all about?"

Jesus responded, "**I have come that my joy might be in you and that your joy might be full**." When we are practicing our joy, we are drawing closer. When we forget our joy, we are falling away. Both our son and his wife are wonderful practitioners of joy, and faithful workers in their church.

First, via Wave Theory, Set the Happy Example

The first, most natural and efficient way to share these enlightenment games with our friends and family is to do so by example, *i.e.*, quietly, or maybe giggly, by osmosis, teaching the value of happiness via a *contact high*! Our happiness *is* contagious. Our peace is contagious.

When we practice our own peace and joy as a daily discipline--as something we *start* with rather than something we hope to make happen--those around us can't help but be influenced. We don't need to say a word. In physics it's part of what is known as "wave theory." The waves we generate encounter and influence the waves that others are generating. (Back in the day we called them "vibes.")

So it is our own playing of the enlightenment games--and daily improvement in our play--that is absolutely the necessary first step in sharing them with others. Bottom line: **If we aren't directly experiencing joy and peace, we simply can not share it, or teach it**.

That said, it is also natural, quite useful and generous to share the specific games outright--to talk about the four steps that make up the first two games, and to share our experiments with the timer and with our meditations. We don't have to be obnoxious or evangelical about our sharing. (Happiness can never be used as a club!) It's best to let the sharing happen naturally, spontaneously, lightly. ("I was reading this goofy book and this crazy guy said . . .")

For young children, especially under the age of eight or nine, but sometimes up to the age of eleven or twelve, who have not yet learned to differentiate themselves from their thoughts and feelings (some folks have still not learned this differentiation even at the age of 70) the "sharing by example" is the most direct and compassionate way of sharing these games. Besides, for many of us, **it's the kids who are teaching us**! Most kids already spontaneously engage these games simply because joy and peace really is the natural "backdrop" of being human. **We don't need to teach them how to be what they already are**.

But once kids are able to "think about their thinking," explicitly sharing these specific games is perfectly appropriate. The sooner they learn how to access joy and peace, the more successful they will be. However, beware: once the kids learn the games, they will be quick to ask, in various circumstances, *"Dad, (or mom,) do you enjoy that train of thought? If it's not an immediate and spontaneous yes…"*.

It is helpful, and open and honest for our family and friends to know the "life games" that we are playing. Even if they themselves aren't interested in such games, to be spontaneously open and honest about our own interest is both generous and loving. But we naturally share these games hoping others might also find them interesting and challenging enough to test them out for themselves. When everyone in the household is playing the games—in their own way, of course, at their own speed--or even **if they are aware of the games we are playing, the peace and joy in the house begins to climb**.

The same holds true with our circle of friends. When we are bold enough to share these games, even if our friends don't begin to play, at least they know what's important to us; they know what we value. This helps our friendships deepen and mature or, sometimes, helps us naturally, gracefully go our different ways. For many of us, this sharing of these enlightenment games with our friends will mirror an earlier season in our lives when we shared with friends our pot-smoking, get-high interests.

At the most practical level, however, our own explicit sharing of these games--sharing with others the basic steps that allow us to directly access peace and joy--**such sharing will greatly quicken our own play**. The more we share, the better we get at sharing, but also the better we get at practicing, playing the games.

Friends and family, as they learn the practices, are generally going to challenge us—challenge our understanding, our commitment, our very peace and joy. It's like playing tennis--we're not going to get better until we take it onto the court and actually play against another player. Playing these games, however, there are no losers! Everybody wins.

Sharing at a Professional Level

As mentioned, in my day job I was a stop smoking (tobacco) coach for our local county Health District. I loved it. I was able to share these games all day every day in one-to-one and small group sessions with a wide rainbow of people, most of whom started off as strangers. (By the way, my experience suggests that **sharing these games with strangers is much easier than sharing them with friends and family!**)

Our program worked on a sliding fee scale and we received direct referrals from local medical clinics, including a large local clinic for low income folks, so I worked with people up and down the social and economic scale. Although at a professional conference I did give a little talk entitled *Why Rocket Scientist's Still Smoke*--why bright, self aware, socially and educationally adept people still smoke--research shows that most current day tobacco smokers have less education, are less economically successful and tend to come from more troubled family backgrounds. That tended to be the case with the salt of the earth clients that showed up for our program.

So how do the Potless Pot High games "work" for people in these less than optimal circumstances? Not surprisingly, they tended to help them *immediately* improve their lives. Here's an example:

One of my clients--I'll call her Ellen-- was a mother of four sons ranging in age from 22 to 32. One son, alas, was in prison, and the other three, after various forays into the wider world, were all still living at home--her home. She also had a live-in boyfriend. When she first came to see me she was the only one in the household with a steady job--she worked in the kitchen of a nursing home where she had started off, fourteen years before, in housekeeping. Everybody in her house smoked, and they did so indoors. She did have grandchildren in the area, but the boys, alas again, were estranged from the mothers. Her seeing her grandchildren was sporadic.

Ellen was not a woman given to outward exuberance, sentimentality or even much laughter. For her, life was tough and she had determined to be even tougher. When I remind people that the most loving thing they can do for themselves and all those around them is to enjoy their own happiness, such a simple reminder often comes not only as a welcome surprise and breath of fresh air, but sometimes as a life-saver. And when I point out that practicing peace of mind is in fact a very *practical* thing for us to do, and healthy, and wise, and that we practice peace of mind only when we are at peace with the thought trains we are riding, at peace with the stories we are telling, the simplicity of such a strategy can be exactly what the person needs to put herself back on solid ground.

Part of the good news is that Ellen did quit cigarettes shortly after we started working together, and after I had shared the first two games. (She was ready. I have learned not to take credit for clients who quit smoking because then I have to take blame for those who don't!) Quitting smoking was something Ellen wanted to do, and **practicing these games basically gave her permission and space and power to do what she wanted to do anyway!**

When Ellen woke to the simple lesson that enjoying her happiness, her peace was her *right*, and it was also in fact the most important and most loving thing she could do for herself and for all those around her, she found a natural strength and inner firmness she hadn't previously known. After her own quitting of smoking, she quickly recognized that she did not enjoy having her family smoke, especially indoors. Since she was the one paying the rent, and since she had just quit smoking, she was within her natural rights to ask the others to smoke outside. (I encouraged her to use her stop smoking coach as an excuse for the new rule--make *him* the bad guy! Joy always leads us to the right solution in these matters.)

Her home is now (mostly) smoke free.

How We Think About Our Lazy Bum Kids

When Ellen shared with me her worries about her sons being "lazy bums," and would probably never find work or homes of their own, I gently asked her what she enjoyed to think about these things. It became clear to her that her own thought trains (*"they'll never amount to anything"*) could be one of the factors keeping her sons insolvent. **And if she wanted her sons to change their own ways of thinking, didn't it make sense that she herself might lead the way by changing *her* own thinking?**

I encouraged her to write down on paper what she enjoyed to think about her sons, what she was most at peace thinking. (Yes, this is a valid part of the stop smoking process. Stress with children, after all, is often the excuse that smokers use to go back to smoking.)

The basic reason I call it the "Freedom Game" is because we are *free to think what we enjoy to think* about those we love (or anyone else) ***in spite of the evidence***! In fact, we can think what we enjoy to think without any evidence at all!

Isn't this what we would want from others, and especially our own family? To have them think about us in ways they enjoy, or at least in ways that didn't cause them inner angst, anger or turmoil?

Here's the rule: We can think about others in the way we want others to think about us! And most especially when we think about our family and friends.

No More Family Black Magic!

Way too often we inadvertently practice black magic--thinking dark thoughts, thinking what we don't enjoy to think, over and over, with great feeling--against those we love most! Having shared these games face to face now with many hundreds of people, I know from firsthand experience that our biggest challenge in playing the games will almost always come from those we love, our closest family and friends. After all, these are the folks with whom we have the most history, and who have the most opportunity to tempt us into riding thought trains we don't enjoy to ride.

Without even trying (and sometimes by trying!) our family often tempts us to jump on trains of thought that we don't enjoy to ride, about them and their relationships and circumstances and how they are acting in the world. But this is how we love them: by *not* yielding to the temptation to jump on that train. We love them by *not* yielding to the temptation to think un-peaceable thoughts about the circumstances and relationships of those we love and cherish.

In my last session with Ellen she took three more "Freedom Game" cards to share with her sons. (I write out both the Freedom Game and Peace Game on small cards so that people can carry them around.)

"Make it easy," I suggested to Ellen. "Say something like, *Here, look at this. Can you believe what my stop smoking coach teaches*?" It's fair to come in the back door in sharing these things with our families—if that approach leads to more peace and ease.

At Peace With (Our Thoughts About) Our Teenagers

Another example: A friend/client who had three teenage sons came to me one day quite exasperated with her second son, who had once again fallen into trouble with both the school and the local police department. "I just don't know what to do with him," she groaned.

"Are you at peace riding that thought train?" I asked. (I can be a nut about this approach.)

"No, I'm not, obviously," she replied.

"Just for fun," I suggested, "if we want to play the peace game, let's take option b--*choose to be at peace with the thought train with which a moment before we were not at peace*. Can you be at peace with the thought, *I just don't know what to do with him*? That does, after all, seem to be the case."

I could see her considering this option-- to be at peace with her quandary--and simultaneously could see the tension starting to drain. "Yes, I can be at peace with this thought."

We talked some more, and it became clear that she might at some point even share this thought with her son--that she didn't know what to do with him. But it had to be an honest sharing, without an ulterior motive. We both saw that if she was not enjoying such a thought, or at least at peace with this thought, then such a statement would quickly become an accusation, or a plea for him to change.

As we talked more it became clear, once again, that the *content* of the thoughts she shared with her son was not nearly as important as the tone or quality of her thoughts—whether she came from a place of peace, (which is another name for love) or a place of upset. And again, the most loving thing she could do for herself and her son was to stay in her peace, her joy. It was the only way to help him find his own peace and joy.

As she left that day she accidentally gave me one of the highest compliments I have ever received in my work with others. "Oh good," she said, off-handedly, as she was walking out the door. "I can go home now and love my son again."

On the surface it might seem that when we give the highest priority in our lives to experiencing more joy and peace that we could end up being a doormat to those around us as we endeavor to stay in peace and joy. Curiously, my experience would suggest just the opposite. When we recognize the *necessity* of authentic peace and joy in our lives—indeed, the life-saving, health enhancing, wealth creating, integrity building, relationship nurturing effects of authentic peace and joy--we are less likely to ignore or "excuse" any unhappy conditions or turmoil which arise in our experience. We are quicker to deal with such conditions, such turmoil, just as we are quick to deal with a pot boiling over on the stove

As we discussed in some detail in Chapter 8, practicing our joy and peace is not just a matter of "positive thinking." **Some days we enjoy to say *yes* to our kids, or**

our parents or friends or colleagues at work, and some days we enjoy to say *no* to the exact same request. As heretical as it might sound, the only "consistency" we truly need in our parenting, or friending, or family relations is consistency in love, in peace and joy. What this looks like one day may be completely opposite what it looks like the next day. We can trust our joy, our peace, our love to guide us in all our affairs. Again, one day we may enjoy to say *yes*, the next day we may enjoy to say *no*. **It is our *joy* that we can trust to guide us in all our affairs.**

By the way, by practicing the Potless Pot High games, Ellen gained the strength to insist that her sons get jobs, start paying rent and do the dishes! The boyfriend also started pitching in his share.

In the next chapter we'll look at how this same principle unfolds in regard to how we relate to and arrange our physical surroundings--our home, our work space, our vehicles. We'll see that our joy, our peace leads us to artfully transform our outer living spaces to reflect our inner ease. It's much easier to be high and stay high in such environments.

And speaking of easy, this whole thing has been easy so far, yes?

Chapter 15

Pot-less Paraphernalia

How to turn all our spaces
into mellow, easy-living *get-high* sanctuaries

"A comfortable house is a great source of happiness. It ranks immediately after health and a good conscience." ---Sydney Smith

During the heyday of the hippie movement folks would sometimes dedicate particular rooms as "get high" rooms, with cushions and flowing curtains, groovy lights and wonderful sculptures (and sound equipment, of course) chosen to enhance the get-high experience. We wanted to magnify our happiness. We were working, in our own naïve way, to create heaven on earth. It's a worthy cause.

Of course, because of the "attention wandering" nature of the high experience itself--and because we were all simply being human--it was hard to keep us confined to a single room. And again, because of the nature of the high experience itself, and because we were human beings, we weren't consistently of the mood to keep these rooms in the pristine order that we hoped might lead to "higher consciousness." And then once again, due to the nature of the get-high experience and being human, most of us were not so professionally or economically adroit that we could afford to dedicate a whole room in our homes or apartments to just getting high. "Life happens" and so the get-high rooms eventually became the storage room or the baby's room or the office or the TV room.

And come to find out, as we've already discussed, it is not *where* we are that *makes* us happy. The good news is that we are *already* naturally, natively happy, already peaceful, no matter where we are. Peace and happiness are our basic nature. And we are learning to express our basic nature in an infinite number of ways, in *every* room of our home and work environments.

Again, being high, clear and spunky is not a part-time job that we experience in just one place but not another. This is a 24/7 opportunity!

First, The Inner Environment

By engaging the Potless Pot High Games we are basically "redecorating," reorganizing and upgrading our inner environments, our inner homes (where we hang out!). We are simplifying, beautifying our inner realms, bringing heaven to earth.

Once we recognize that enjoying our happiness, practicing our peace really *is* both the most loving thing we can do and the most practical thing for ourselves and all those around us, we begin to consciously entertain only those trains of thought that we most enjoy to ride and with which we are most at peace. As we engage such simple "inner environmental" practices we will find ourselves *spontaneously* moving in our outer environments in ways that likewise magnify our basic peaceable nature.

Put more simply: as we practice our peace and joy our home and work environments spontaneously become more organized, more welcoming, more efficient. Although such reorganizing and upgrading happens spontaneously, we can also enjoy to do it consciously, intentionally, making our home and work environments into "playing fields" for these get-high, stay-high games!

So here are five basic guidelines for transforming our homes and work spaces into happy and peaceable environments for playing the enlightenment games:

1. The means and the ends are the same. To end with peace and joy expressed outwardly in our home and work environments we must *work* with inner peace and joy; we must (*we get to!*) start with peace and joy. In other words, it is the *process,* and not the end result that truly makes a difference in our environments. **Guideline number one is always, "Stay in your peace, stay in your joy**." Following this guideline, the end results will effortlessly take care of themselves.

Example: When I was a kid, my dad, who had not learned to enjoy yard work, thereby unintentionally made our Saturday yard work into an unhappy battleground. Although our whole family spent many hours working in the yard (it seemed to me like many *many* hours) our yard was never a source of peace and pleasure for our family, and, alas, never more than mediocre in its appearance. And the memories of our childhood yard work inspire my brothers and me to hire lawn crews here in our maturity.

On the other hand, our grandpa had somehow learned to *love* to work in the yard and garden. It relaxed him. Made him whistle. His lawns and gardens were beautiful. **The means and the ends are the same**, now and forever!

Example Two: We've all known people for whom a clean house is the most important thing in the world, and these folks generally believe this priority should be the same for everybody else. One woman went so far as to keep a vinyl plastic covering on her couch to keep it clean. A clean house may *express* peace and happiness, but it does not *cause* peace and happiness.

We can go into other homes and though they may not be spic and span clean, they are nevertheless somehow orderly, peaceable, pleasant to be in. The "vibes" with which we work are what we are installing into our homes and work environments. We can't fake it.

So again, Guideline Number One: Stay in your joy, practice your peace. The means and the ends are the same.

2. Cleared outer spaces help elicit cleared inner spaces. It's pretty obvious that war tends to make clutter—or, more specifically, bombs making rubble out of city blocks and mortars smashing through roof tops and tanks crashing through garden walls all tend to make clutter. When the bombs stop and the peace returns (may it happen quickly!) we naturally want to start clearing the clutter. How many parents have told their kids, "Your room looks like a war zone!"

Pot tends to lead us toward more peaceable living, at least in the beginning. (Again, it's not coincidental that so many anti-war "peaceniks" are also pot users.) Although I have friends who enjoy to get high and then clean and tidy their living spaces, this is not generally the mood that pot leads us to, nor does pot lead to consistently focusing on such activity.

Stoned or not stoned, clear, open spaces are generally more peaceable than crammed and cluttered spaces. In Buddhist retreat centers, for example, simplicity and open spaces are generally quite obvious. Thousands of years of tradition have shown that the Buddha nature is most easily expressed in such simplicity, such "emptiness."

Again, let's be clear: Open spaces, clutter-less counters and desks and floors and shelves do not *make* the peace. The peace is already there, here, inside of us. And we can be peaceable and enjoy our lives and homes and other's homes regardless of the interior decorating going on. Nevertheless, it is fairly obvious that a simpler, less cluttered environment is easier to live in and work in than one that is not so. And once again, let's observe that this is not--can never be—a final goal that we are moving toward so much as it is an every day *process* that just makes sense. We can stay happier, more peaceable, more efficient and easy in a less cluttered environment. Clear outer spaces *do* help elicit clear inner spaces.

Example: My wife will generally not start cooking in a cluttered kitchen. She'll spend ten minutes or more to clean the kitchen before she dirties it again. It's just a more peaceable way of cooking! (My own cowboy approach to cooking is a bit less demanding.)

Example two: We've all known people in both corporate and governmental organizations who keep their offices very clean, tidy and organized but are basically pains in the butt to work with, while others with more cluttered and pile-based offices are more fun and sometimes more practical. Nevertheless, isn't it generally the case that those whose offices look like a war zone are often less efficient, less capable and less relational than those who have more orderly environments? There are exceptions to this, of course. But the general rule . . .

The "director of communications" in one of the agencies where I worked had one of those "war zone" offices. His excuse was he always had so much to do, and all the reports and brochures and communications from every department had to go through his office. Maybe true, but it seemed for a "director of communications" he was the least communicative of anybody there. He was often rushing to meet his deadlines, often very slow to respond to requests and was basically a "bottleneck" in the flow of communications for the entire organization. Was it because he had a messy (disastrous) office? Probably not--but the office reflected his state of mind, and his work practices. Which comes first, the chicken or the egg? Here, we know: un-peaceable, cluttered mind frames generally lead to cluttered, un-peaceable environments.

Still, it is fair to go in the other direction. We can clear our spaces to help clear our minds!

3. **Brief moments count!** Many brief moments of attention to our environment add up, and are usually (though not always) better than long hours or no moments of attention. Obviously, we have many more brief moments available to us than long hours! And we can observe that our environments, both at home and work generally get cluttered and disorganized due to our "brief moments" of inattention and hurriedness rather than because of long periods of chaos and mayhem. (Though we occasionally experience these, too!) Doesn't it make sense to use the same method—brief moments—in upgrading our environment that we used to degrade it?

Example: I've discovered that the time it takes for me to make my bed in the morning is generally two minutes or less--brief moments. And yet the difference between a "made bed" and an "unmade" bed whenever I (or anyone else) walk into the bedroom is huge! (Okay, not huge. But it does make a difference!) Yes, granted, peace and happiness do not depend on whether a bed is made or unmade. And yet, a made bed expresses (a little) the orderliness of the total universe. A brief moment expresses eternity! (And by the way, researchers have found that a made bed prepares one for a better night's sleep!)

Example two: I had a client who loses stuff--big stuff, like full boxes of nicotine patches--in her *van*. "It's in there somewhere," she would say. How peaceful is that? I've discovered that a brief moment of removing the trash, receipts or papers from the car as I exit—or sometimes when I enter --helps keep the car environment a little cleaner, and thus the traveling a little more peaceable. Noticeable? In fact, yes, it is. Does a clean car lead to total enlightenment? What would Jesus' car look like?

4. Use the timer. Brief moments can be extended by the timer, which is a magical environmental transforming device. As we discussed in depth in Chapter 10, when we "frame" a project with the timer, dedicating ten or fifteen minutes, more or less, to that area of our lives, we are, on the one hand, much more likely to begin a project that we've been putting off and, on the other hand, end the project easily. Cleaning the garage or the garden beds or the storage closet often seems like a major project, necessary though it may be. Giving ten minutes to such projects, or 20 or 30 or 60 minutes, lets us see a close-at-hand *end* to the chore, so we are much more likely to begin. We've already dedicated a whole chapter to this topic, so no need to go into further detail here.

Example: As a lifelong writer I inadvertently accumulated over many decades literally dozens of cardboard boxes of old notebooks, manuscripts, partially started projects, published and unpublished articles, essays, stories, poems and great ideas that I wanted to get to "some day." Organizing all this junk seemed an overwhelming, undoable project. So over the past several years, before beginning my ("*timer-based*!") daily writing stint, I dedicated ten minutes each morning (yes, just ten minutes!) to going through a box, throwing away the detritus and then cataloguing and filing the "keepers" into filing cabinets. What can I do in ten minutes? Not much. In a week (six days) that's an hour. In a year, that's fifty hours. In two years, that's a hundred hours. I'm within a couple of boxes of having all my "life's writing work" catalogued and filed.

5. If it doesn't generate good vibes, ditch it. We can pretend that every day we're going to take an acid trip. In such an altered state we are very (very!) open to our immediate environment. We see our dishtowels in a new way. Our coffee cups reveal their artistic elegance—or lack thereof. Some articles of clothing have good vibes, some bring up crummy memories. Yes, saints and sages have shown that we can be peaceably happy in a prisoner of war camp or in a mountain cave or sitting on a dung heap. It's not the outer environment that determines our basic nature. Yet we can also be easy on ourselves, ordinary and kind, simply by removing from our environment all the junk that is just that, junk--and keep what makes us grin. This is not a one time event. This happens in brief moments of daily awareness.

Example: At one point I noticed that every morning as I sat to read the daily newspaper, I'd get bummed out—un-peaceful, unhappy. I was either unhappy with the low quality of the "Mc-Chain" paper itself, or unhappy at what was being reported, or unhappy about how it was reported. And the newspapers would stack up and I'd think of the trees . . .So (in a brief moment) I called and canceled my subscription.

Curiously, I'm much better informed now (via web sources) than I was with a newspaper subscription; a few more trees are still standing and my mornings are more peaceable. Piece by piece we bring peace to our world. (And RIP to our daily newspapers!)

Example two: Grandma's chair might have been her pride and joy, and very expensive to recover, but it's not all that comfortable, the colors don't blend and nobody ever sits there. We can donate it or Craig's List it, even before we have a replacement. The open space will be welcome!

Okay, granted, again, just getting rid of grandma's chair does not in itself necessarily lead to being high, clear and spunky. But it doesn't hurt to clear the space.

In the next chapter we'll head in the other direction and explore how our happiness, our peace and joy are not dependent on *any* of our time/space circumstances. All time/space circumstances must of necessity arise in awareness itself. We'll bring the whole playing field together (so to speak) in our fifth game, the Awareness Game.

Chapter 16

Game Five: Thoughts, *Schmotts*

Getting High, Staying High Is All About <u>*Awareness*</u>

"If you want to find God, hang out in the space between your thoughts." --- Alan Cohen

"People assume that [the Freedom Game] is about thoughts," Dr. Almayrac once said. "But it's not. In fact, the game is about joy."

The same holds true for the Peace Game. When we first begin playing these games we naturally assume they are about the trains of thought we're riding. (*Am I at peace with this train of thought, am I enjoying this train of thought, yes or no*?) When we take a moment to inquire whether we are enjoying the trains of thought that are moving through our consciousness, or whether we are at peace with these thought trains, such inquiry spontaneously moves us back *away* from our thought trains in order to examine them.

When we are watching our thoughts, asking whether we are at peace with them or enjoying them, where are we standing? Where are we asking from? Aren't we standing in awareness itself? And if awareness itself can quickly determine whether or not we are enjoying a thought train, or are at peace with a thought train, *(if it's not an immediate and spontaneous yes it's a no*), then peace and joy must be inherent qualities of awareness itself, not confined or limited by thoughts.

It's *Awareness Itself* That Is Inherently High

Again, this might seem like philosophy, or theory. It's not. It's *observation.* Philosophy or theory won't get us high—won't bring on the grins--until we personally begin practicing, playing the games!

Again, how these games—these observations--function is by gently pointing us back, again and again, to our own innate *peace and joy* which in turn point us to awareness itself. The games, whether they be the quick games of brief inquiry or the more formal games of meditation and the timer, move us back into resting, standing as simple awareness. As we mature in our inquiries our attention spontaneously moves away from the particular thought trains we are riding in any given moment, back to the innate peace and joy against which and in which we are monitoring the trains of thought.

Another way of saying this is that such games, such inquiries help us *differentiate* ourselves from our thinking, differentiate our ever-present essential nature (peace and joy!) from the passing forms and images that make up so much of our everyday lives.

Richard Moss, MD, in *The Mandala of Being* suggests that "What plagues humanity is that, though we all have minds, very few of us understand our own minds. Said in another way, we are poorly differentiated . . .Well-differentiated people tend to see more points of view and have less need to limit or dismiss those of others . . .To differentiate ourselves is to keep stepping back from any strongly held opinion or self-definition. It is to be able to exercise the power of awareness . . . " (p.74).

Moss observes that the ongoing political and cultural wars are consistently perpetuated by people who are strongly and habitually identified with their personal thoughts and feelings, with their personal belief systems, their points of view. When such thoughts, feelings or belief systems are challenged—when their points of view are challenged--these people take such a challenge as a direct threat to their own personal identity, *i.e.,* a threat to their own existence! This is how a particular "belief system" or point of view that someone holds becomes literally a life and death issue!

This clinging to thought trains, to points of views, to belief systems is what leads to the verbal bombing of media pundits and the literal bombing of abortion clinics, the Trade Towers and Baghdad mosques. Most people have not yet learned to differentiate their true natures (ever present, alive, peaceable and harmonious awareness, *i.e.,* love) from their acquired cultural belief systems.

But the times they are a changing.

All Feelings, Thoughts, Sensations Are *Points of View*

Candice O'Denver, founder of the international Balanced View and Great Freedom community, suggests that *all* thinking, feeling, sensing and experiencing can be understood simply as various "points of view" arising in awareness itself. She echoes other ancient and contemporary seers when she points out that awareness itself is our essential nature, rather than the personal points of view that arise in awareness.

O'Denver points out that our culture-- every culture-- educates us to *identify* with our points of view, identify with our momentary thoughts, feelings and sensations-- and thus to identify with limited, ever-changing, never-stable phenomena. Such false identification is the basis of suffering.

We started this book by observing that the get-high experience has functioned in most of our lives as a way to help us end the suffering, if only momentarily. (Again: When the Buddha was asked *what is enlightenment,* he responded, "Enlightenment is the end of suffering.")

Suffering comes from rigidly identifying with our temporary points of view, most often expressed in particular and various trains of thought. Since we are inherently so much more than our momentary, temporary "train of thought," when we identify so narrowly with such a particular thought train, it is akin to forcing a size nine foot into a size seven shoe. It can be done, but it hurts!

Another way of understanding the get-high experience is that it offers a way of physiologically "releasing" our various habitual trains of thought—taking our foot out of the cramped shoe, standing back from our strongly held identifications. (One common agreement amongst all stoners is that Congress needs to hold a literal "joint session" to help them modify and enlighten their rigid, unworkable trains of thought!)

When we look carefully at the high experience we can see that what makes it attractive to so many people is that it is a way of temporarily *differentiating* ourselves from our everyday thought streams, feelings or perceptions. Indeed, this a big part of why marijuana often works so effectively as a medicinal pain reliever. **Getting high allows us to release our psychological grip,** which spontaneously relaxes the physiological grip. We stand back a bit from our ordinary points of view, jump off our unwelcome thought trains. Suddenly our world looks new.

And yes, let's admit, pot also lets us stand back from even our seemingly rational, practical points of view such as, "I really should finish high school!" Or, "I should mow the lawn." "I should finish that project." Sometimes when we get high, and enjoy new points of view, our old points of view--at least for the moment--no longer hold our interest, *i.e.*, no longer make up our *identities!* (*I am so much more than a 12th grader, or a lawn mower!*)

Timothy Leary's encouragement to "Turn on, tune in and drop out" was an accurate description of what often happens. When we turn on we tune in to something larger than our old points of view, our old thought trains, and thus these old views, these old identities no longer "fit." We drop out of them, just as we drop out of the size seven shoe when we find a larger, more natural and thus more comfortable world view.

So we might ask, if pot helps us stand back from our thought trains, our old identifications, why do our perceptions--thoughts, feelings, sensations--often seem *heightened* after a bowl or two? Why do we get *excited* about our thoughts, feelings, perceptions? Why do our thoughts and feelings often seem more interesting, more intense after toking up?

Seeing the Forest AND the Trees

It is just this *standing back* from them that allows us to see them in a new light, to get excited and enthralled with sights, sounds, perceptions that previously (or later) might seem rather mundane. In our ordinary daily lives we tend to get lost in the trees. Getting high helps us see the forest. As we discussed in previous chapters, when we get high the inner gates stay open longer, we see more, and we see it from a slower, more relaxed (alpha and theta) state, rather than the *hurry-hurry* beta state. It's good, and even healthy on occasion to stand back from the trees, the daily rush, in order to see the forest, the wider picture.

And yes, sometimes, let's admit, if we smoke too much weed too often we become slackers, lose sight of our "tree nurturing" responsibilities. After all, it is generally (though not always) quite useful, quite practical to actually finish high school, or college. The lawn does need mowing. Reports generally need to be turned in if we want to keep our jobs.

Nevertheless, it *is* useful to stand back from the trees in order to see the forest. Otherwise, as has been demonstrated time and time again amongst the "straight" population, we can attend to the *busy-busy* tree work our whole lives--getting reports done, mowing the lawn, getting the next certificate of accomplishment--and then suddenly plop over into the grave without ever having fully appreciated, enjoyed, savored the delicious experience of simply being alive. With such a life, the epitaph on our grave might read, "*She stayed very busy*!"

Or worse, we can get so deep into the trees--into our own narrow points of view--that we strap dynamite around our waist and blow ourselves up in the marketplace. Or we're so dominated by some personal point of view that we decide we should cut off all communication with our kids, or folks because they are not in line with our points of view! Or we simply miss the delicate, dynamic beauty of our everyday life in blind pursuit of tomorrow's promises.

So how do we balance the two—the wider view and the daily chores, the forest and the trees? We do so by taking up the "life games" as outlined in this book. We start by paying attention to what we are thinking, consciously (bravely) deciding to think what we enjoy to think, or at least what is most peaceable to think. Generally, we start playing these games just for the fun of playing, and maybe to test the theory that enjoying our happiness really *is* the most loving thing that we can do for ourselves and all those around us, and that practicing peace really *is* the most practical thing to do for ourselves and everybody else.

For most of us who play these games, at some point what starts off as theory becomes a real-life *experience:* **we suddenly *know* that enjoying our happiness *really is* the most loving thing we can do. Practicing peace really *is* completely, absolutely practical!** The games become real.

A Matter of Life and Death

With such direct experience of the power of peace and joy (even though it sounds corny) we spontaneously get more serious about this stuff. *We recognize that how well we play these "life games" is truly a matter of life and death,* or at least a matter of life and boredom. How well we play the games makes the difference between suffering and not suffering.

Paradoxically, when we directly experience the absolute necessity of joy and peace in our lives, and bravely determine to make the experience of peace and joy the *highest* priority every day, both at work and on the weekend, then the temporary expedients to peace and joy--be they drugs, sex and rock and roll or vocational ambitions or political or religious extremism-- no longer truly satisfy. We begin to demand the real McCoy.

In other words, at some point we don't want just *hints* of enlightenment, hints of the end of suffering. We don't want to settle for just a taste. We want the whole banquet. Every day. All day.

What could possibly satisfy such a wanting? The whole banquet--every day, all day. Is there anything in the entire universe that could possibly offer such fullness? That would not go stale? Not grow old? What would it look like? Feel like? And if we found it, how could we not lose it?

Awareness Itself Is the Get-High Stuff, Pearl of Great Price

This is where the old story comes in of the man who searches the world over for treasure—the pearl of great price--and then finds that it was all along in his own back yard. What can give us the whole banquet, all day, every day? What *already* gives us the whole enchilada? It's so simple, so obvious, so close to home that we tend to overlook it.

Yes, of course—as the start of this chapter should have indicated--the jewel of great price is awareness itself. Awareness itself is the first energy, our basic identity, our natural self. Awareness itself is that in which all thoughts and feelings arise. Awareness is what thoughts and feelings are *made* of!

When we allow ourselves, moment by moment, to release our grip on all of our thoughts, feelings, sensations, circumstances--all of our points of view--and simply *enjoy* awareness itself, be at peace with awareness itself, we've come home.

Awareness itself is what is always here, always with us whether we are happy or sad, stoned or straight, active or passive. Even in sleep, awareness is present, though without an object.

Come to find out, awareness itself is the supremely potent "get high" substance that is always available, never runs out, never gets stale, and is impossible to abuse! It's what we've been looking for all along! And, great news, we already have a magical, self-renewing stash of the stuff!

We're not talking here about something esoteric or mystical or hard to find. We're talking about plain old ordinary, every-day awareness. The "good stuff" was all along hiding in plain sight. Again, awareness is what our thoughts are made of. Awareness is what our feelings and sensations are made of. We were just so wrapped up in our thoughts and feelings that we didn't recognize the "field"-- the stuff-- in which they were arising. (Until we got stoned!)

And it is not only are our personal thoughts, feelings and sensations that are made out of awareness. Come to find out, according to the latest scientific discoveries, when we look deep into the nature of matter itself, *everything* in the entire universe is apparently made out of awareness. For example, as mentioned in a previous chapter the quantum physicist Amrit Goswami from the University of Oregon wrote a book on quantum physics entitled, "*The Self-Aware Universe*." What quantum physicists have discovered is that at the smallest micro-level of matter, before energy becomes either a particle or a wave, *intelligent awareness* is present. It's the same awareness in which the universe itself is swirling, resting.

So when we turn our attention to the presence of our own daily awareness, we are tuning in to the fundamental energy of the universe. *That* is powerful get-high stuff!

So how do we do it? How do we tap into our own daily awareness to get high and stay high? Or more accurately, how do we tap into our awareness to end the suffering, end the effort to shove the size nine foot into the size seven shoe? How do we tap into awareness to access our joy, our peace, whenever we want, wherever we are?

To use the words of Candice O'Denver, we do it in "brief moments, repeated many times until it becomes constant." We simply move our attention off our momentary points of view, our various trains of thought--release our grip on whatever thoughts, feelings, sensations or experiences may be arising in the moment--and rest in awareness itself, which is always already present. It is awareness itself in which these thoughts, feelings, sensations and experiences are arising.

When we move our emphasis to awareness itself, rather than to the objects arising in awareness, we cease pushing the river. We effortlessly carry on with our ordinary daily lives—we continue to chop wood, carry water—yet we do so as *awareness itself* rather than as some momentary object or relationship or sensation or personality that is arising in awareness.

To repeat: We soon come to recognize that our momentary points of view--our momentary thoughts, feelings, sensations or experiences--are *made* of awareness itself. It is clinging to these momentary thoughts, feelings, sensations and experiences that "weighs us down." We "get high" simply by releasing these inner weights that we habitually carry. We drop all anchors, our *attachments* to the *objects* of awareness. Doing so, we naturally, spontaneously grin! And then grin again. And again.

Making It Simple

Okay, let's bring this high sounding discussion home, make it easier, more practical.

Are you aware that we've come this far? Of course you are.

If you will notice, the *content* of your awareness may have changed since the first chapter—the concepts and formulations may have changed--but the awareness itself has *not* changed! **Our simple (yet magical) awareness is the "background" on which, in which everything arises and then falls away, never leaving a trace. This is our "home" position.**

The English potter and mystic, Rupert Spira, in *The Transparency of Things,* offers a wonderful metaphor. He writes,

> "If our attention were now to be drawn to the white of the paper on which these words are written, we would experience the uncanny sensation of suddenly becoming aware of something that we simultaneously realize is so obvious as to require no mention. And yet at the moment when the paper is indicated, we seem to experience something new.
>
> "We have the strangely familiar experience of becoming aware of something which we were in fact already aware of. We become aware of being aware of the paper.
>
> "The [white of the] paper is not a new experience that is created by this indication. However, our awareness of the paper *seems to* be a new experience.
>
> "Now what about the awareness itself, which is aware of the paper? Is it not always present behind and within every experience, just as the paper is present behind and within the words on this page?
>
> "And when our attention is drawn to it, do we not have the same strange feeling of having been made aware of something that we were in fact always aware of, but had not noticed?" (p.xiii)

The Zen Master Huang Po when asked "what is enlightenment," responded, "Your ordinary mind." Awareness is here with us every day, in us, around us, but most of the time most of us are so wrapped up in the *objects* of awareness, the relationships, the words on paper that we overlook the most potent "get high" substance in the universe!

We don't have to *do* anything to get high, clear and spunky without weed! Awareness is already present. We've already been inoculated. We just have to let it do its magic. We don't have to do anything to get high and stay high except that we *do* have to stop bringing ourselves down!

Let me suggest that the first four Potless Pot High Games gently prepare and guide us to directly experience the reality of our own "pre-thought" presence, which is attention itself, or awareness itself. Again, we can easily observe that when we play the Freedom Game or the Peace Game we spontaneously step back from our thought trains to gauge whether or not we are enjoying them, or whether we are at peace with them. This is like stepping back from the words on paper to see the paper itself.

The Timer Game allows us to direct attention--awareness--into particular frameworks, regardless of thinking momentum. Meditation is another way of stepping back from the false identification with the cognitive circus, or as the Buddhists call it, "The monkey mind." This fifth game--what Robert DeRopp called "The Master Game"--points us to what was there all along: our own simple daily awareness.

When we examine our own daily awareness we discover that it is in essence invisible, formless. Awareness has no fixed borders, no time, no space, no anchors at all. A little bit like an acid trip. Such a state--which is no state at all, but rather that in which all states appear and disappear--is what the pot high points to, and offers a glimpse of, but does not allow us to *live* there.

We are pointing here to the natural state—awareness itself--also pointed to by such contemporary teachers as Ekhart Tolle, Byron Kadie and Wayne Dyer, and by the best of traditional teachers both east and west.

This is a simple observation-- that at the root of all our experience is awareness itself and that awareness itself is the basic life energy. As we rest in this basic life energy, life takes care of itself. We discover we are always in the right place at the right time, with the right people, saying and doing the right things, with a natural, spontaneous grin!

The Simplest Practice

This may sound goofy, and perhaps too easy, but the most direct "practice" I personally have yet to discover for quickly returning to rest as awareness itself is to simply ask myself, *"Who am I?"*

This of course is the classic "inquiry" recommended by both eastern and western sages and saints down the centuries. Asking the question, *"Who am I,"* freezes, or at least slows the mental and emotional process for a moment, allowing awareness itself to look out--and in--at what's happening, and *who* is happening.

Here's a vital point: The *answer* to the question *"Who am I?"* is not as important, or powerful, as the act of posing the question itself. **The question takes the *questioner* out of the moment's "identity**"--whether it's an identity around washing the dishes or preparing an annual report or talking with friends--to the richness of *what is.*

The basic question *"Who am I?,"* although sufficient in itself to return us to pure awareness, and thus to feeling high clear and spunky, can take on many forms. *"What am I?" "Who is it that is walking here?" "Where am I?" "How am I?" "Who is it that is feeling this way?"*

Again, the *form* of the question is not as important as the *posing* of the question. By turning attention around to look at the "questioner," the presence of awareness--the "medium" in which and by which the questioner exists--becomes more apparent.

Many other questions have been used to bring the questioner to a clearer sense of the presence, or Presence, of the wider being. *"What would Jesus do?"* also operates to freeze-frame, if only for a moment, the small personal identity to become aware, again if only for a moment, of the larger, deeper picture.

Over the years, my own path has led me to use many, many different types of "mind stoppers"--or a least "mind changers"--pot being only one of those types. I've also used a wide variety of meditations, including mantras and various chants, breathing exercises, koans and inner visualizations, as well as foreign travel and card games and mountain hikes and business deals, all in the search of the "permanent high."

Here in my white-haired maturity, I find the simple question, *"Who am I?"* is the simplest, most direct, most efficient means to the momentary relaxing of identity and the enjoyment of being. And isn't that what getting high helps us do--relax the citizen, busy-busy day-life identity in order to simply enjoy *being itself*?

How to Suspend the Inner Monologue

When we ask, *"Who am I?"* and take a moment to honestly observe who or what it is that is functioning in this moment, the inner monologue is spontaneously suspended, at least for a moment.

At root, **it is only awareness itself that is aware of itself.** So this simple question often brings awareness itself back into the foreground (just like alpha moves in front of beta, *i.e.*, just like getting high!)

When I ask the question (*who, or what, am I?*) I often feel my shoulders spontaneously relax, and/or a deep release of breath, *i.e.*, coming home, coming back to what is true in this moment. Much like a righteous hit of weed (again, without the head rush.)

Isn't it clear that when the inner monologue is suspended, we are still present? Or at least *something* is still present. That ordinary *something* is awareness itself. When the monologue starts up again, that ordinary *something* is still present. Awareness is still present. The monologue tends to get so noisy and demanding that awareness itself is forgotten, ignored. Thus, ignorance--ignoring--of our basic state, the natural state

.

Again, many, many traditions exist that offer other techniques for returning to the experience of awareness itself. Many, many teachers and researchers down through the centuries have tested and refined these techniques. In the

Eastern traditions this topic is particularly focused on by teachers of "advaita," now being brought to the contemporary west by teachers of "non-duality." (See the bibliography at the end of this book).

In Western traditions this focus on awareness is particularly dominant in the teaching of "contemplative prayer." When Jesus said, "I am the light of the world," might he have been pointing to the light of his own deathless awareness? Is his awareness the same awareness we all share? When we return to awareness, do we return to the light?

We don't have to make it complicated. **When we rest as awareness, we rest as love.** As awareness itself we are spontaneously open, peaceable and kind. We are spontaneously high, clear and spunky. We are our natural selves, naturally high.

As awareness itself we still chop wood, carry water, go to the grocery store, get high or not. So, the question arises, as awareness itself, do we ever need to smoke weed again? For that discussion, let's go to another chapter.

Chapter 17

Does This Mean I Can't Ever Smoke Pot Again? (Of Course Not.)

Will I Want to? Will I Need to? (Yes and No.)

"The only way to deal with an un-free world is to become so absolutely free that your very existence is an act of rebellion. "

--- Albert Camus

When we are identified with our thoughts, feelings, sensations, hopes and fears, pasts and futures--identified with our thought-trains, our points of view--we are chained to such identifications, such viewpoints. Such identifications hold us down, hold us in place, are a drag on our daily lives. In other words, **we keep ourselves from being high**.

Now, let's don't go too fast here. As adventurers in consciousness we need not be just armchair travelers, accepting such statements--*we keep ourselves from being high*--as just an interesting theory. As adventurers, we are free to verify the veracity of such statements in our own ordinary lives.

Do our own familiar points of view, daily thought-trains actually weigh us down, keep us chained, keep us from staying high? If so, then this is an important discovery, a radical observation. It's worth testing out.

On the other hand, rather than bringing ourselves down by identifying with our thought trains, if we instead simply rest as awareness itself, identify with awareness itself, we find ourselves free of those thought chains; we are, free of not only our own points of view and trains of thought but also free of other people's points of view, their thought trains, just as the sky itself is not bound by what is rising in it in that moment. Thought trains and points of view will continue to rise up in awareness. Fireworks may fill the sky offering colorful lights, smoke, explosions and the smell of gunpowder. The inner crowd will *ooo* and *ahh*.

But all such "arisings" inevitably fall away, eventually leaving the sky as clear and clean and as pristinely present as it was before the fireworks rose up. A spring day on the present-day Gettysburg battlefield shows us the truth of this.

And even though we too *ooo* and *ahh* along with the crowd--we too are human--we can spontaneously grin at the empty sky before the show, grin at the fireworks, grin again at the return of the empty sky. **An inner grin is our "background" stance**, our white paper upon which the words are written. Identified with awareness itself, we are free of that which rises up in awareness.

Which means we are free to *ooo* and *ahh* and yet we are just as free to go for a walk or take a snooze. Identified with awareness itself we spontaneously do what is most appropriate in the moment. Nothing is forbidden, yet nothing is ordained. We *are* the empty sky, completely at ease, at rest, open, yet not clinging.

So, relative to smoking pot--yes of course we are free to smoke pot if and when we are so moved. (But only in Colorado or Washington, or off-shore in international waters, so as not break any silly prohibitionist laws.)

As should be fairly obvious by now, this is clearly not a traditional "recovery" book where, once we see the light, we are then obliged to never again touch the wicked substance that has supposedly been the bane of our existence. What is offered in this book is a radical, yet very gentle, approach to the whole enchilada. Once we truly see the light we discover that we are truly, inherently free to dance and sing and shout and move about in whatever way the moment inspires.

Dropping our thought trains--or more precisely, our *identification* with our thought trains--we are suddenly more alive, more spontaneous, more free and easy than we have ever been. We are at rest in the moment. Nothing's obliged, nothing's forbidden. And yet . . .

We are no longer so moved, or determined to *change* our thought trains, our ordinary points of view, which is what pot tends to do. We are *already* high, already clear, already spunky, thank you very much. We don't need to change *anything*! It's as if we're eating a piece of chocolate cake and someone comes up and asks if we want a piece of chocolate cake. *Uhh, no thanks, already have some . . .*

Viva la Revolution!

Standing as awareness itself--recognizing that awareness itself *is* our fundamental nature--we spontaneously express deep integrity. The first Webster's definition of integrity is "adherence to moral and ethical principles; soundness of moral character; honesty." The second definition is, "The state of being whole, entire or undiminished. "

When we recognize our deepest nature, integrity is not something we *try* to do. It's something we *are*. We are already whole, already complete, in need of no amendments. We spontaneously act with moral character, according to moral principles.

Most every pot user has had the experience of being so high that **we forget to smoke the rest of the joint**, or the bowl. We don't *need* to smoke any more. We're already stoned, already grinning, already where we want to be.

Is it possible to live our lives in that state where we are *always* right where we want to be, already grinning, don't need anything more, thank you very much? It doesn't mean we don't go to work, don't do the laundry, don't mow the lawn. It doesn't mean we don't join the revolution and overthrow the oppressors.

Rather, it means we are happy to go to work, we're not fighting with the laundry, we're at ease mowing the lawn. We are content to devote the rest of our lives to the revolution, overthrowing the oppressors. In such a state wouldn't our work be done more gracefully, the laundry more efficiently, the lawn mowed more artfully? Is it possible to stop a revolution of those who are completely content to devote their lives to radical change, no matter what fireworks may arise? *Viva* such a revolution, and such revolutionaries.

Addicted to Pot?

So okay, what if you're addicted to pot, and you use it to extremes? Maybe you know it's interfering with your work and school and family life. You know your use is out of balance. You're not happy smoking so much. But the urge, the cravings keep coming back, and you can't resist them. What do you do?

Basically start *seriously* playing the games outlined in this book. They worked for me. They can work for you.

Make your joy, your peace, the most important thing in your life. Yes, you once found joy and peace in smoking weed--we all did, some still do. So be it. But let's say you're not at peace with smoking so much. Let me remind you:

Practicing peace of mind is the most practical thing you can do for yourself and all those around you.

You are at peace when you're at peace with the thought trains you are riding.

So don't freak out about your pot smoking. Don't chew on thoughts you don't enjoy to think. Give yourself some time. Don't make a huge problem of your pot smoking. Lighten up.

Practicing these games, as outlined in this book, will lead you more and more to simply *forget* to smoke, again, just like you sometimes forget to finish a doobie because you're already cruising.

Start cruising--not only when you're high, but when you're not high. Enjoy yourself. Be at peace with yourself. Be radical: Be brave enough to just ride the thought trains you enjoy to ride, or with which you are at peace, no matter what others may be thinking. And again, you're free to decide to enjoy a particular thought train, or at least be at peace with a particular thought train with which a moment before you were not at peace.

Smoking pot heavy duty every day is a season that many folks fall into. It can end as easily, naturally and as effortlessly as it began!

What *Not* to Do:

So here's what not to do, at least in my view. **Don't turn yourself into a "drug rehab" program**, unless you're addicted to other substances that could create major physical withdrawal problems. A drug treatment program will most likely treat your pot smoking as an "illness," a disease which needs to be cured. It's not.

You might have some other issues that could use a helping hand--we can all use wise outside advice and support in our lives. And we can be humble enough to ask for it. Sometimes our other physical, emotional and mental issues lead to our extreme pot smoking. *But the pot smoking itself is not an issue*!

Your pot smoking is an adventure you're on that, we can assume, had many interesting and fundamentally healthy things to teach you. So maybe for you the adventure is not so much fun anymore. (Nobody likes to feel chained to any behavior. Nobody likes to be addicted.)

So keep your eyes open for the next right step in this adventure.

Obviously, if you bought this book and you've read this far, this is exactly what you are already doing. So again, just chill. Start practicing the games outlined in this book with great curiosity . . . see for yourself if what I suggest actually works. (If these games help you stay high, clear and spunky without weed, I'd like to know. If they don't help, I'd like to know that too!)

I know very well that this is heretical advice. To simply suggest, *take it easy, just chill, enjoy your life,* completely contradicts what 95% of the rest of the "treatment" folks would tell you that you should do. With great respect to what the other treatment folks are doing, I beg to differ.

I'm an old guy. I've worked in depth over a long period of time with folks suffering under the heaviest of addictions (to heroin, meth, alcohol, tobacco, etc.). I know, from sad, direct, in-your-face, break-your-heart experience that most of our current addiction treatment models simply don't work most of the time for most folks. Sad, but true.

Not only do they most often not work, they often create more problems than they fix--by installing a "disease" model in the psyche that is supported and affirmed by the ruling elite. Don't buy into it. That's my advice.

A Gentle, Practical Approach to Pot Addiction:

My own experience is that by practicing these games my own pot addiction gently, spontaneously fell away. I still smoke pot on occasion, when appropriate. But I easily go months and months without even thinking about it (except when I'm writing this book!) I don't jones for a smoke. I'm already cruising.

I wrote a book for tobacco smokers--***How to Stop Smoking in 15 Easy Years—A Slacker's Guide to Final Freedom***. If you're finding yourself very troubled with your pot smoking, you might want to give that book a try. The first homework assignment in that book, found on the first page, is:

Just Be Who You Already Are and Enjoy Your Smokes.

The reason this is the first homework assignment is that most smokers tend to beat themselves up all the time about their smoking. And it doesn't work. They get caught in a loop that can take years, decades, to get out of. So in order to get free of the habit. they have to stop doing what they've been doing, which is beating themselves up about it.

As might be expected, my encouragement for smokers to first enjoy their smokes (as their first step in quitting) was neither generally understood nor welcomed by many other stop-smoking professionals. Most were aghast at such advice. Nevertheless, I'm happy to report that my work with tobacco smokers trying to quit had one of the highest success rates in the country--as determined by independent evaluators checking in with my clients seven months after starting to work with me. **Joy really does work to free us of unwanted habits**!

I've noticed that habitual pot smokers who are trying to quit also, tend to beat themselves up about their habit, (most often *after* they've toked up!) Here's the deal: **Beating ourselves up about how we're living our lives is not the most graceful way to refine our lifestyle**! Sure, it can be done--we can change our lives by beating ourselves up--but it's the hardest, least efficient way to do it.

Following our peace and joy, resting in simple awareness, is the most graceful way to bring more joy and peace into our lives. Here why: The means and the ends are always the same. Have I said it enough?

So, bottom line: **Resting as awareness itself, we can smoke weed or not. We are truly free** to live our lives moment by moment in harmony with the moment's artistic demand. And yet, resting as awareness itself we already feel full, complete; we don't need to go anywhere other than where we are, right here, right now. We *forget* to smoke weed, for months on end! And then years on end.

We're already high, clear, spunky, thank you very much.

We outgrow pot just like we outgrow high school or our first job after college. After we've been practicing these games for a while, intentionally enjoying our happiness, consciously practicing our peace, finally resting as awareness itself, we most often discover the pot high is too temporary, too scattered and has too little *lift off* power. Even the best weed reveals itself as somewhat silly. Once we've been to Paris, Lubbock seems a little tame.

Nothing wrong with Lubbock, of course. And if we happen to be in that part of Texas . . .

The intent of these games is to help us be easily, naturally, spontaneously free to live our lives in elegant, appropriate response to the momentary circumstance.

All of life's experiences are freely available to us. Again, "nothing is forbidden," as Dr. Almayrac often said. When we recognize the happiness that is already present, the peace that is already ours, our actions become spontaneously honest, compassionate, and infused with great integrity. We may smoke pot or not. But we don't *need* to, ever again.

Such is the result of relaxing into our natural selves, our natural being. This moment already contains the whole enchilada. We spontaneously grin, chop wood, carry water, do the laundry and foment revolution.

What a great planet to have as our playground!

Speaking of fomenting revolution, when are we going to bring down the "Great Wall" that separates the people from their birthright--the obvious, natural right to smoke or not smoke--or make brownies or cupcakes from that silly little cannabis plant?

Shouldn't we be working to legalize the stuff? We need another chapter.

Chapter 18

The Question of Legalization (No Question at All!)

"An unjust law is itself a species of violence. Arrest for its breach is more so." --- Mohandas Gandhi

I'm happy to report that Colorado, where I live for most of the year, was one of the first two states (the other was the state of Washington) to legalize pot. Let's hope and assume these are the first two dominos to fall to cause a chain reaction of similar legalizations across the country. (When other states see how many millions in taxes are being collected, it could happen very quickly!) Such legalization is, in my view, long overdue.

Speaking of Absurd Laws

In the early 1900's in the small town where I live an ordinance was passed that made it illegal to carry a lunch box down the main street. The town fathers didn't want "that" kind of man (who carries a lunchbox) walking the streets of our fine town!

Such absurd laws are not unusual. We humans seem to want to legislate how other folks should live, and think and feel. We pass such laws for our own presumed safety (because we are at times secretly fearful of our neighbors) and for the safety of those who apparently can't see what's good for them, can't see what's right and wrong. Obviously, what seems to be quite proper and reasonable in one era, or area, shows itself to be quite silly and narrow given wider experience.

For example, at one time:

- It was an act of treason to place a postage stamp bearing the British monarch upside down.
- In France, it was forbidden to call a pig Napoleon.
- In Ohio, it was against state law to get a fish drunk.
- In Indonesia, the penalty for masturbation was decapitation. ("*Off with his head*?")
- In San Salvador, drunk drivers could be punished by death before a firing squad.
- In the UK, a man who felt compelled to urinate in public could do so only if he aimed for his rear wheel and kept his right hand on his vehicle.
- In Florida, unmarried women who parachuted on Sundays could be jailed.
- In Kentucky, it was illegal to carry a concealed weapon more than six-feet long.
- In Vermont, women had to obtain written permission from their husbands to wear false teeth. (All of these are from the *Times Online*, August 15, 2007)

And the list goes on and on.

But obviously, not all laws are bad. We do pass good laws amongst us that help us to live more reasonably, more justly and harmoniously with each other. (It is the law that we stop for a stop sign!) Nevertheless, what seems reasonable in one era--as the above list shows--loses its reasonableness in another era.

As a stop smoking coach I'm quite familiar with the way the pendulum swings over the centuries in regards to tobacco laws. For example, in the early 1600's, King James, who hated smoking, forbid the importation of tobacco. So people immediately began smuggling it and growing their own. (Sound familiar?)

Since King James was at war with the French, his advisors suggested he make tobacco legal but levy a huge tax on it--thus paying for the war and simultaneously encouraging people not to smoke because it would be so costly. This is still a well-known and widely used tactic around the world, though its effectiveness is slight.

About the same time King James was passing his laws, Sultan Murad IV in Turkey, fearing that the type of person who would smoke tobacco was the type who might plot against him, made smoking tobacco a capital offense. He would run a pipe through the nose of those caught with tobacco and ride them on a donkey to the town square to be beheaded. Any Turkish soldier caught smoking would have both his arms and legs broken and then his helpless body put in the field between two opposing armies. (When people say we should "get tough" on smokers, is this what they mean?)

At one time, tobacco was outlawed in both China and Russia. In Russia, a person caught with tobacco could have his home and possessions confiscated and be sent to Siberia. In China, tobacco smuggling was a capital offense. Is it just a coincidence that today the highest per capita smokers in the world are in Turkey, China and Russia?

Relative to pot laws, I know, I know--I'm preaching to the choir. Most of us interested in the topic of this book probably already agree that the laws against pot are our equivalent of the Berlin Wall.

In the U.S. the current federal laws against pot originated in the 1930's after Prohibition was repealed, primarily as a covert political maneuver to keep in place the federal bureaucracy that had been built—and funded--to fight "the war on alcohol." A wise, beautiful and deeply researched book detailing these issues is *Drug Crazy: How We Got Into This Mess and How We Can Get Out* by Mike Gray.

Looking at the origin of pot laws, it is clear that the current laws against pot came about as a result of a system infused with groundless fear, deep racism and open bureaucratic self-service. At best, the laws are based on proven fallacies. This makes the laws themselves fallacious. At worst, the laws are an attempt at centralized thought control. These laws need to come down.

Being Potless Makes Us Braver Advocates!

My experience suggests that once we actually stop smoking the stuff, or at least once we are no longer *addicted* to it, we become much more vocal about legalizing it. And, fortunately, we also become more clear, more confident, more precise and insightful about the obvious necessity--and inevitability of legalization.

Again, as I write this, my own state, Colorado, and the state of Washington have, through popular vote, recently legalized pot. It's been a long time coming, and way overdue. It is time for the whole country to be free of the not only harmful, but violent and counterproductive laws against marijuana.

This book is not the place to get deeply into the "whys" of legalization. Again, I assume we are talking to the choir here. Nevertheless, it doesn't hurt to refresh the picture. The following observations are based on over 25 years of empirical studies from around the world.

First, regardless of the supposed harm of marijuana ingestion, it might be reasonable to ask whether the laws against pot use actually work. They don't.

Close to 100 million Americans say they have tried pot. Over twenty-five million admit to smoking in the past year. (But wait, it's against the law!)

Regardless of whether marijuana is harmful or not, the laws against it don't work to curb its use, or initiation or sales. Both here in the U.S. and around the world the experience of cities, counties, states and countries that have "loosened" or abandoned their pot laws show no significant increase in teen use or adult use.

Amsterdam, the most famous "pot city" in the world where one can go into a state licensed coffee house to purchase and smoke the world's widest variety of marijuana, has about the same percentage of cannabis users as any major city in the U.S. And actually a *lower* percentage of teen imbibers!

According to the *British Journal of Psychiatry*, "The Dutch experience . . .provides a moderately good empirical case that removal of criminal prohibitions on cannabis possession (decriminalization) will not increase the prevalence of marijuana [use] or any other illicit drug . . ."

The same experience--no major increase in use--was found in Portugal when pot was decriminalized. And countries such as Spain, Italy, Belgium, Croatia and Switzerland have all decriminalized the use of weed without having any of the horrific results that the anti-pot folks fear. In a nutshell, **the laws against pot are not keeping the barbarians at bay. In fact, such laws are *creating* the barbarians**. (Think Mexican drug cartels who slaughter innocent people to protect their trade.)

In the same way that Prohibition led to the rise of violent organized criminal gangs who were trafficking in alcohol, the current drug laws have led to the rise of violent organized criminal gangs trafficking in pot, cocaine and other illegal drugs. Pot becomes a "gateway drug" primarily, if not only, because it's been forced into the same underground economic network as the more dangerous substances.

What Did Abe Lincoln and George Washington Say?

So what do these violent and unworkable laws do to our relationship with our government? What have they done?

Again, this is not the place to recount the tragic and widespread personal, familial and economic suffering that has occurred because of the failed "War on Drugs." An overwhelming majority of legal scholars, sociologists, political scientists, psychologists and family counselors all agree that this ill-conceived policy has created untold-—and unnecessary--havoc throughout all levels of our social structure.

Lewis Korn wrote, "The final test of civilization of a people is the respect they have for law." George Washington wrote, "Laws or ordinances unobserved, or partially attended to, had better never been made."

Abraham Lincoln agreed when he wrote, "Nothing is more destructive of respect for the government and the law of the land than passing laws which cannot be enforced." Dan Simmons observed, "Laws have a bad habit of being ignored or abrogated when societal push [meets] totalitarian shove."

From all the evidence, **it is not marijuana itself that is destructive but the laws against marijuana**--"the totalitarian shove"---that are tearing apart the fabric of our society.

But Isn't Marijuana Bad for Us?

No. It's not.

As we've discussed throughout this book, pot has its limitations. It is not the ideal enlightenment vehicle that we might hope it would be. It can lead to temporary lethargy, dropping out, and/or a messy room. But both the physical and psychological effects of marijuana on the body are relatively benign, and in some instances quite beneficial. Let's be clear:

- Marijuana is non-toxic. Nobody has *ever* died from an overdose of marijuana.
- Marijuana does not kill brain cells.
- Marijuana is not worse for the lungs than tobacco.
- Marijuana does *not* cause crime.

And on and on. **All unbiased investigators into the physical, mental, emotional, and societal effects of marijuana have come to the same conclusion: The criminalization of marijuana is a mistake.**

And the studies supporting the use of marijuana for medicinal purposes are incontrovertible. Even though the government has consistently blocked research into its medicinal use, the research that has been allowed shows that it consistently ameliorates nausea and vomiting, it stimulates hunger for those undergoing chemotherapy or AIDS treatment. It's been proven to decrease eye pressure and thus immensely useful in treatment of glaucoma.

Marijuana has been used successfully in the treatment of spasticity in both Parkinson's and Multiple Sclerosis, for a variety of movement disorders, for asthma (it's a "bronchial dilator"), for inflammatory bowel disease, migraines and fibromyalgia and to provide pain relief from various cancers.

Although its use as a pain reliever has been disputed by some authorities, the direct experience of tens of thousands of people suggests that for many people it does, indeed, relieve many kinds of pain. (See our discussion in Chapter Nine.)

Again, to deny the relief that marijuana has proven to offer those who are suffering is itself a criminal act. Henry David Thoreau wrote, "If the machine of government is of such a nature that it requires you to be the agent of injustice to another, then, I say, break the law."

The laws against medicinal marijuana are indeed unjust. But so are the laws against recreational use.

Get Tough = Get Stupid?

Even those who have been paid by the lawmakers—and law keepers—to investigate the nature of cannabis have come to the same conclusion. Under President Richard Nixon the National Commission on Marijuana and Drug Abuse (The Shaffer Commission) recommended that marijuana use **not** be made a crime. President Nixon rejected the evidence of his own scientists and insisted on his "get tough" policies.

According to the secret White House tapes, Nixon equated marijuana use with a Jewish conspiracy to dominate the world, with communism, homosexuality and perversion. Because of his irrational prejudices millions of people have been arrested and countless careers damaged, finances ruined. This is unjust.

Those who blindly support the irrational laws might be seen in the same light as the hired guards at the Berlin Wall, "just doing their job." They need to resign. The Bud Wall needs to come down.

Drop Out of School, Get Involved

Again, my experience has been that once I stopped regular use of marijuana I became a much more vocal advocate of its legalization, starting with decriminalization. It's as if we have a brutal, narrow-minded totalitarian principal running the local high school. It's hard for the high school students themselves to do much about it because the principal has instituted harsh, punitive measures against anyone who speaks up or resists his rule.

Once out of high school, however, we are much more likely to speak up, work openly and vigorously with others to have that bully removed. A number of brave, high-integrity and level-headed organizations are working to change the marijuana laws, based on a deep well of sound scientific research and irrefutable sociological studies. Organizations such as NORML (National Organization for the Reform of Marijuana Laws), MPP (Marijuana Policy Project) and the Drug Policy Alliance (DPA) are doing much to advance sanity and decrease the violence and unfounded paranoia around marijuana.

And then there are the wonderfully goofy, outrageous and in-your-face "opposers" of the marijuana laws--both individuals and organizations--who dance and laugh and wear outlandish costumes, play their music loud, insist on freedom *now*. So be it. The times demand---or at least allow--for such expression.

We can engage the cause and do so joyfully, peaceably, reflecting our deepest nature. With such an approach, we are unstoppable.

What we don't need to do--and what is counter-productive to our cause--is make "enemies" of particular people, particular personalities who are the "guards" at the wall, or maybe even the captains of the guards. Public apologists for the current marijuana laws are not our personal enemies. As Gandhi pointed out, "It is quite proper to resist and attack a system, but to resist and attack its author is tantamount to resisting and attacking oneself. For we are all tarred with the same brush and are children of one and the same Creator."

It's useful to remind ourselves that our "adversary" is the *system of law* that is broken, not the people who are serving the system. And more particularly, more personally, our basic adversary is the anger, the fear, the irrational despair that the system tends to evoke in ourselves and others. Going beyond such personal negative states is the enlightened approach--the Potless Pot High approach--to moving beyond the current societal suffering. Going beyond such states is what makes for a true revolutionary!

The enlightened approach, the Potless Pot High approach to life is what this book has been about, yes? Let's finish up our time together, (with just one more chapter) and then get on with enjoying our lives, get on with bringing peace to earth.

Chapter 19

Conclusion: We're Only Just *Beginning* to Get High!

The Evolution of Human Beings Is an Evolution of Consciousness

[Your daily] Mind is consciousness which has put on limitations. You are originally unlimited and perfect. Later you take on limitations and become the mind. ---Ramana Maharshi

Since you've come this far in this book (even if you just flipped to the end!) it signifies that you, too, are a natural "explorer" in human consciousness (and potential revolutionary!). It was your own curiosity that has fueled your journey here. You were curious about whether there really is a way to get higher, clearer, spunkier without weed. That's a worthy quest. It isn't over yet.

It was the same native curiosity that first took so many of us into experimenting (and experimenting and experimenting) with pot and other mind-altering substances. Such curiosity is a healthy thing. Yes, curiosity may have killed some cat somewhere, but it was rare. And curiosity. May have killed or wounded a few of our friends and acquaintances who were curious about "one more hit." (No one, let us remind, has ever died of an overdose of pot!)

But curiosity also drives evolution. Curiosity opens new frontiers. Curiosity cures disease. Curiosity makes fortunes. Or simply makes the day a little brighter, easier, more fun. Refreshed curiosity is one of the first "fruits" of returning to and resting in awareness itself. Returning to awareness feels as if we've suddenly come more awake, more alive, more alert, though in fact we're just returning to what has been here all along. (Doesn't that sound like a pot high?)

This has been a fun book to write. I've been compiling the Games and other content for many years through personal research, professional training and simple trial and error. Curiously, and not surprisingly, putting it all down on paper has quickened my own personal practice, opened new doors, made my day life clearer, spunkier, more relaxed and grin soaked. So for this I get to thank the reader!

Here's the take-away message: **you—me, we--are *already* higher than we ever dreamed possible. And clearer and spunkier. The *feel-good* from the get-high was already in there, *is* already in there. Its basis is simple awareness itself**. What weed allows us to do--for a moment, temporarily, in a somewhat awkward and inefficient way--is to change our points of view within awareness, stand back from our habitual thought-trains in order to to see the world anew. This is not a bad thing, even if how we do it is somewhat awkward and inefficient.

Again, even though weed as a means to an end tends to be a bit awkward and inefficient and in the end somewhat repetitive, most of us end up being quite grateful for the presence of this magical herb-- and for the lessons, blessings, friendships and space trips that it has brought.

Just as most of us were grateful for 8th grade. But it's time to move on.

Well, okay, pot was, is, maybe a bit more exciting, mysterious and life-changing than 8th grade. But the metaphor is appropriate. The get-high from pot can be a season in our lives--be it long or short--but there's something more profound than 8th grade, more true about us and more fun that is already closer to us than our own breathing. No sense repeating 8th grade time and time again.

Our experimentation with pot--and/or other drugs—is an experiment in consciousness. **We have rightly been attempting to free consciousness from the false constructs imposed not only by cultural programming but also by biological necessity**. It's a bit like the early natives who wanted to explore the wide ocean. Their small canoes could not take them to the farther shores. New vehicles--better ships--needed to evolve.

Our experimentation and exploration is itself a happy, peaceable affirmation and confirmation of what Ekhart Tolle called the dawning of "The New Heaven and New Earth." (And of course, St. John used those exact words 2000 words earlier!) Something new *is* happening on this planet--something is evolving, waking up--that has been millennia in gestation!

It is this "new heaven and new earth" that the pot high gave us a glimpse of. Thank goodness! Through smoking weed we found new ways of thinking, feeling, being. But now we want more than a glimpse. We want to *live* there! Here. Such a bright presence--heaven on earth--is our birth right. So why do we keep coming down, keep getting thrown out of the garden?

Unconditioned Awareness = Unconditioned Love

Come to find out, when we just relax, even for just brief moments, the heaven on earth that is our birthright reveals itself to be always and everywhere already present. **It is the magical substance of awareness itself that is always already present . . . yet so simple, obvious and non-threatening.**

We don't have to light it up. Awareness is already lit. We don't have to inhale. Awareness is already inside. We don't have to hold it. Awareness holds us. We don't have to exhale. Awareness is already outside.

We live and move and have our being in this magical substance of awareness. Unconditioned awareness is unconditioned love. It's our very nature. When we rest in our nature, it brings on the grins, in us and all those around us.

We're just beginning our journey together. As we learn to enjoy our simple, yet magical awareness, we also learn to enjoy each other more. And then we discover that there is no other. Awareness is a single magical presence. It's our common ground. Our common being. (The ground of being!)

So here, one last gesture: Let's both take a toke of the ground of being, of our *own* being. (One toke is all we need.) Being/awareness makes us high. Makes us clear. Keeps us spunky.

Forever and ever and ever.

Sweet, eh?

Let me know how you're doing, and what games *you're* playing!

bear@potlesspothigh.org

"I see the poem or novel ending with an open door."

--- Michael Ondaatje

Suggested Reading

A Few Books from My Favorite Wise Guys, and Gals:

Rather than being confined to one particular path, many of us are on what I call "the book path." What freedom! Here are a few of the most influential, for me, off the top of my head.

Spira, Rupert: *Presence: The Art of Peace and Happiness - Volume 1 and 2* (Non-Duality Press, 2011) Rupert is my "go-to" guy—*numero uno* teacher--when it comes to direct perception of reality. His books are transformative. His presence and teaching even more so. Check him out, however you can.

Godman, David: (editor) *Be as You Are: The Teachings of Sri Ramana Maharshi* by Sri Ramana Maharshi (Author**),** (Penguin, 1985) Ramana Maharshi might be considered the Godfather of contemporary gurus. David Godman is his consigliere. Any book okayed by David Godman is a worthy read.

Nisargadatta Maharaj: *I Am That*, Translated by Maurice Frydman , Sudhakar S. Dikshit (Editor) I've read this book four times and am working on my fifth. It's the real goods.

O'Denver, Candice: *One Simple Change Makes Life Easy* edited by Balanced View **Team** I love this lady's teachings, even though, sadly, she is allowing a cult to grow around her. But check out her Balanced View teaching. It's simple, and it works.

Suggested Reading (cont.)

Katie, Byron : *Loving What Is: Four Questions That Can Change Your Life* (Three Rivers Press, 2002) I selected this book by "Kaitie" just because it was handy. Any of her books will do. She will help you come unstuck, no matter where you are.
Gangaji, *Hidden Treasure: Uncovering the Truth in Your Life Story* (Jeremy Tarcher/Penguin, 2011) Gangaji offers a worthy d introduction to Papaji, and all the gurus who came from him. Again, I picked this book at random. Any of hers will do. u
MacCoun, Catherine: *On Becoming an Alchemist: A Guide for the Modern Magician* (Trumpeter Cooks, 2011) One of the best "transformation" books I've read in the last twenty years, and I've read a gazillion of them. Funny, down to earth and revolutionary.
Spangler, David: *An Introduction to Incarnational Spirituality* (Lorian Press, 2011) What a breath of fresh air is David Spangler. He is a maverick, who says its okay—and even spiritual-- to be in the flesh! This is a good intro to him.
Tolle, Ekhart: *The Power of Now: A Guide to Spiritual Enlightenment* (New World Library, and Namaste Publishing, 1999) If you haven't yet read Ekhart Tolle, you're in luck, because you still have that pleasure in front of you. Get over your prejudice. Give him a gander. He's being honest.
Carse, James P : *Finite and Infinite Games: A Vision of Life as Play and Possibility* (The Free Press, 1986) This is a classic little book that helps put life and its games in perspective. Play it!

Other of my favorites: ***The Vedas, the Tao Te Ching, the Torah, the Bible, the Heart Sutra, Hitchhikers Guide to the Galaxy,*** but then . . .where to stop? The book path goes on and on, thank goodness. The right next one always pops up, doesn't it?

Suggested Reading (cont.)

About the Brain and the Use of Weed and Other Drugs

I won't comment on these books. I've said enough about these things in the preceding book. Here are a few of my sources.

Tart, Charles: *On Being Stoned: A Psychological Study of Marijuana Intoxication* (Science and Behavior Books, 1971)
Fehmi, Les: *The Open Focus Brain: Harnessing the Power of Attention to Heal Mind and Body* (Trumpeter, Books2011)
Robbins, Jim: *A Symphony in the Brain: The Evolution of the New Brain Wave Biofeedback* (Grove Books, 2008)
Ram Dass: *Be Here Now* (Lama Foundation, 1974)
DeRopp, Robert S: *The Master Game: Pathways to Higher Consciousness* (Gateway Books, 2002)
Weil, Andrew: *The Natural Mind: A New Way of Looking at Drugs and Higher Consciousness* (Houghton Mifflin, 1973)
Huxley, Aldous: *The Doors of Perception: Heaven and Hell* (Harper Perennial Modern Classics, 2004)
Castanda, Carlos: *The Teachings of Don Juan: a Yaqui Way of Knowledge* (University of California Press, 1968)
Gray, Mike: *Drug Crazy: How We Got into This Mess and How We Can Get Out* (Random House, 1998)
Fox, Steve: *Marijuana is Safer, So Why Are We Driving People to Drink?* (Chelsea Green Publishers, 2009)

Contact the Author:

Please Feel Free to Contact Me with News, Insights, Questions, Complaints, Compliments, or Invitations:

Bear Jack Gebhardt
bear@potlesspothigh.com
606 Hanna St. Fort Collins, CO. 80621

May peace and joy and a consistent, spunky clarity be yours everyday…

--- *Bear G.*

Made in the USA
Las Vegas, NV
11 December 2022